LANGUAGES IN BRITISH BUSINESS

An Analysis of Current Needs

Edited by Stephen Hagen

Newcastle upon Tyne Polytechnic Products Ltd

in association with

The Centre for Information on Language Teaching and Research

ISBN: 0 948003 42 1

Newcastle upon Tyne Polytechnic Products Ltd
Library
Ellison Building
Ellison Place
Newcastle upon Tyne NE1 8ST

Tel: (091) 235 8148 or (091) 232 6002 Ext 4148

Centre for Information on Language Teaching and Research
Regent's College
Inner Circle
Regent's Park
London NW1 4NS

Tel: (01) 486 8221

CONTENTS

i

PART II: THE VIEW FROM INDUSTRY AND TRAINING PROVIDERS

Foreword

by Sir Hugh Campbell Byatt, KCVO CMG
Chairman of CILT

The arguments for a greater awareness of British business of the importance of languages have been voiced both from conference platforms and in print for a number of years. It is good to see that, at last, British business is beginning to act on such messages and to secure the benefits which our international competitors have understood for years. The availability and importance of English still clouds our perceptions and cushions our linguistic disadvantage, but we need to remind ourselves that young business men and women, whether they be from Germany, Japan, or Korea, are not simply learning English, but also the languages of their customers. For example, some 300,000 Koreans are learning Japanese, according to recent figures. Nearer to home, the Single Europe Act of 1992 will harshly expose any lack of language skills – and equally important, any lack of cultural awareness of our European neighbours – on the part of British business.

There are, however, grounds for optimism, as this book shows. British business is taking languages more seriously, and in many cases developing proper training and recruitment policies. Our education system is now placing greater emphasis on languages for communication, and it is Government policy that the dominance of French in our schools and colleges be countered by a planned increase in the learning of other languages. Beyond school, the current development, with pump–priming from Government, of a network of Language Export (LX) centres is accelerating the progress towards a proper matching of training needs against services provided.

I commend Stephen Hagen's compilation to the attention of any business with an eye not just to expansion but to survival. Its message is clear and should be acted upon.

PREFACE

This book sets out to evaluate, firstly, firms' own perceptions of the role languages play in business today and, secondly, to provide examples of good company practice developed by industry, for industry, in response to these language needs. Surveying a large enough sample of firms to ensure a national picture has been a major, time–consuming task which has come about thanks only to the efforts of the individual contributors. Many of the contributors have carried out the work in their own time and on a shoestring budget. The limited backing for the project has been drawn from a variety of sources; sometimes from within regional organisations, sometimes from the institutions where the contributors work. Where appropriate, contributors make the position of funding clear in their own acknowledgements.

The articles in Part I generally follow common guidelines on survey methodology. Percentages are given of the complete samples ('N') of foreign–language using respondents in each case, rather than of the total of question–respondents, unless otherwise indicated. Since individual respondents write on behalf of their company, the samples are referred to as 'companies', or 'firms'. For ease of convenience the term 'company' is also taken to include firms which are not incorporated, as well as regionally–based autonomous branch plants. Respondents asking us to refer to 'Head Office', or who duplicated information from other branches, were excluded.

More data have been collected than could be published here, but the publication clearly raises serious issues which need to be addressed by the Department of Education and Science, the Department of Trade and Industry and Local Education Authorities. An on–going centrally funded research study into this whole area of the link between languages and trading performance needs to be quickly established to follow up the valuable work of this project. Comparative studies should also be carried out on a European scale, particularly as 1992 draws closer.

Many of the original articles have been edited to ensure they follow the same pattern in terms of theme, length and results. Each author has had control over data collection and the interpretation of the findings in writing. However, any editorial mistakes in the text are entirely my own. The addresses of respondents have been treated confidentially and therefore do not appear in the publication, though a number of companies have been quoted or referred to as examples of good practice. Some of the information gathered for this publication, however, would not have appeared unless confidentiality had been offered to all respondents.

From the correspondence received, I am satisfied that the evidence in this publication is representative of the state of languages in British industry and commerce today. The fact that certain company–types responded more than others is symptomatic of a greater concentration of need in particular sectors and in firms of a certain profile. There are, however, many firms which remain blissfully unaware of the problem. Hopefully, this publication will bring some insight into the international approach and training practices of the larger, more successful British companies like Rowntree Mackintosh plc and ICI Chemicals and Polymers Ltd.

Finally, I would like to thank Newcastle Polytechnic Products Ltd for its commitment to the publication and especially the care taken in processing the manuscripts, particularly under pressure of time. My thanks also go to Alan Moys of CILT for his help and advice, to Dr James Foreman–Peck of Newcastle University for his useful suggestions, to the Department of Modern Languages at Newcastle Polytechnic for support with administering the Northern Survey, to the Standing Conference of Heads of Modern Languages (SCHML) for their encouragement and, above all, to the authors themselves for their contributions to the project.

Stephen Hagen
Newcastle upon Tyne Polytechnic

LIST OF COMMON ABBREVIATIONS

A, Ar:	Arabic
BOTB:	British Overseas Trade Board
BTEC:	Business and Technician Education Council (Examinations)
Chin:	Chinese
E.A.:	East Anglia
E.M.:	East Midlands
eng:	engineering
Eng:	English
FEU:	Further Education Unit
F, Fr:	French
FL:	foreign language
For:	Foreign
FLAW: Examination	"Foreign Languages At Work" (the scheme operated by the London Chamber of Commerce and Industry for non-specialist foreign language options in schools)
FLUNCI:	"Foreign Language Use in Northern Commerce and Industry" (the acronym of Hagen's study in North East England and Cumbria)
G, Ger:	German
Hum:	Humberside
Int:	International
I, It:	Italian
J:	Japanese
lang:	language
LCCI:	London Chamber of Commerce and Industry (Examinations Board)
LX:	"Language-Export" (name of PICKUP/MSC-funded regional centres for developing language services)
N.E.:	North East England and Cumbria (= the Northern Region of England)
Ox:	Oxfordshire and Thames Valley
Pol:	Polish

Q1, Q2 etc:	"Question 1, Question 2 ..." referring to questions on Hagen's questionnaire in Appendix 1.
R, Russ:	Russian
RSA:	The Royal Society of Arts
Rum:	Roumanian
S.E.:	London and South East England (see Chapter 8)
S.H.:	South Hampshire
Sp:	Spanish
S.W.:	South West England
trans:	translation
TVEI:	Technical and Vocational Educational Initiative
UGC:	University Grants Committee
Yorks:	Yorkshire

INTRODUCTION
Stephen Hagen

The rise of English to its predominant position as the world's leading language has accelerated during the last quarter of this century. It has eclipsed French in the realm of international diplomacy and left German far behind as the first language of science and technology. At the same time there has been a paradoxical increase in the use of languages *other than English* by British industry and commerce. Changing patterns of trade toward non–English–speaking markets have been clearly evident since Britain joined the EEC a decade and a half ago, yet an increasing awareness of changing perceptions about the value of using the customer's language has been much slower in appearing. Only in the early 80s has there been any discernible increase in companies' appreciation of the role foreign languages can play in business success, especially in the new, traditionally non–English–speaking markets of the world. There has been a need for up–to–date statistical evidence on the nationwide pattern of demand for foreign languages in British industry and, in particular, on the link between language use and export performance.

The object of this collection is to make good this deficiency, firstly, by analysing the current language needs of British industry in Part I and, secondly, proposing solutions in Part II. Whereas Part I focuses on data submitted by companies[1] of all types, i.e. by the end users themselves, Part II comprises specific case studies, or models, of successful company practice. Contributors from three large international companies, ICI Chemicals and Polymers Ltd., Rowntree Mackintosh plc and Peugeot Talbot (UK), focus on meeting language training needs and creating multilingual cultural awareness in the company. Robert Taylor (IC Ltd) and Anne Clark (Halton College) are widely known for their success and experience in providing high–quality language training to industry; and Dr Noel Anderson is a staff technical translator for Randall & Partners Ltd., a leading commercial translation group.

Peter Blackburn of Rowntree Mackintosh plc introduces his article, *Languages in a Multinational Business*, with a quotation from Gladstone, emphasizing that Britain's commercial relationship with

European countries is longstanding, even if the common perception of Europe is of a distant, unconnected alien world. The commercial value of a command of foreign languages in these 'faraway lands' was uncompromisingly stated in a study of other countries' trading success by W.S.H. Gaskell in 1897.[2] Significantly, Gaskell's advice on converting prices into the local currency and translating trade literature into the customer's language, rather than inundating foreign consulates with 'unintelligible' English ones, has stood the test of time. Almost the same words were used about British sales brochures in a survey carried out by the British Chambers of Commerce in Europe nearly a century later.[3]

British companies have been able to 'muddle through' in past years, thanks largely to a bouyant domestic market and traditional ties with English–speaking countries, especially those in North America and the Commonwealth. Whilst our share of world trade has been steadily declining down to rough parity with Italy's, the proportion of Britain's exports to the non–English–speaking world has increased. Correlation between languages and trading performance, particularly in manufactures, has been examined in detail elsewhere[4]. What is clear, however, is that Britain's trade deficit in manufactured goods – primarily in the motor vehicle sector, but also in textiles, iron and steel, resins and plastics – would be reversed if more balanced trade could be established with only three countries; West Germany, Japan and Italy.[5] It is not fortuitous that German, Italian and Japanese come respectively second, fourth and sixth in the rank order of foreign languages most lacking in our aggregate sample of British companies. The evidence here tends to support the proposition that 'effective communication in marketing to non–English speaking countries depends on foreign–language proficiency, (rather than) reliance on English alone'.[6] At present Britain relies on non–English speaking EEC countries for about 48% of its export sales (Table 1), an increase of approximately 150% since the mid–seventies.

The key European languages, German, French, Spanish and Italian, are likely to play an increasingly important role in U.K./EEC trade if Britain is not only to maintain its market share, but to expand it. Table 1, for example, shows how Britain's exports to EEC countries greatly exceeds exports to the USA and our older English–speaking markets.

Introduction

The survival of manufacturing in this country will depend on exports to non–English speaking markets: between 1973 and 1983 the volume of manufactured goods imported into the U.K. from European Community members had risen by 300% whereas Britain could only manage an increase of 66% in the other direction over the same period.[7] Other countries have mastered our language and market, but we have not reciprocated to the same extent. This deficiency, moreover, seems to apply to firms all over Britain.

TABLE 1: Principal U.K. Export Outlets

U.K. Exports to:	1985 m.a. in $ 000's	1986 m.a. in $ 000's	% of U.K.'s World Trade	
			1985	**1986**
U.S.A.	1254.9	1274.0	14.8	14.3
Canada	182.8	207.5	2.2	2.3
Australia	148.4	150.0	1.8	1.7
New Zealand	42.9	42.0	0.5	0.5
E.E.C.	4132.3	4284.3	48.8	48.0
W. Germany	966.5	1043.5	11.4	11.7
France	837.4	758.6	9.9	8.5
Netherlands	793.4	664.8	9.4	7.5
Japan	109.4	145.8	1.3	1.6
World	8462.0	8918.4	N/A	N/A

Source: Monthly Statistics of Foreign Trade (OECD)
N.B. m.a. = *monthly average*

Origins And Scope Of The Present Study

Taken together, the thirteen surveys in Part I constitute the first nationwide study of foreign languages across eleven regions of England and Scotland. Data from nine of the regions (see Table 2), namely North East England and Cumbria, West and North Yorkshire, Humberside, the East Midlands, Oxfordshire and the Thames Valley, East Anglia, London and the South East, South Hampshire and the Far South West, are directly comparable. In these cases the questionnaire designed and first tested in North East England in 1984 provided the necessary common framework for matching samples in the nationwide study. The choice of primary stratification of the sample according to region, rather than, for example, company–type

TABLE 2: AN OVERVIEW OF SAMPLES IN NATIONWIDE STUDY

Region**	Year	Total Response	% Using For. Langs (positive respondents)	No. Of Firms In Each Sample ('N') .
Northern Region	(1984)	241	69.7%	168
of England	(1985)	197	76.5%	151
Yorkshire	(1987)	*	*	86
Humberside	(1986)	94	77.7%	73
East Midlands	(1986)	120	87.5%	105
Oxfordshire	(1986/7)	123	71.5%	88
East Anglia	(1986)	122	48.5%	59
South East	(1986)	77	67.5%	52
South Hampshire	(1986)	62	76%	47
South West	(1987)	*	*	37
OTHERS[11]				
West of Scotland	(1985)	177	90.5%	160
Northern Region	(1985/6)	118	60.2%	71
Sussex	(1986/7)	100	53 %	53
			TOTAL:	1150

* missing value

** See Appendix 3 for a comparison of the regional GDP per head

or industrial sector, has been largely determined by the location of researchers and the local availability of funding, or support, for projects with an identifiable regional focus.[8] However, the value of allowing educational provision in languages to take account of regional divergences within a national picture has been previously referred to by Hagen[9] and Coutts.[10] In two of the regions, Sussex and the West of Scotland, different questionnaires were used, so the data are comparable, but not matching, with the other surveys. Nevertheless, both are regionally–based, have the same primary objective of identifying the language needs of local industry and were carried out within the same period – 1985–7.

Certain parts of Britain, e.g. Eastern Scotland, North West England, the West Midlands, the Bristol area, and Wales, do not appear in Part I, largely due to a lack of volunteers at the time the study was launched. However, two of these regions are represented in Part II of the study by Robert Taylor's and Marion Smart's company language–training programmes in the West Midlands and Anne Clark's chapter on supplying the training needs of companies in the North West.

The information content of the surveys have necessarily had to be restricted for the purposes of this publication. Most surveys have yielded more data than could appear here, a few – notably covering Southern parts of England – produced smaller and, in some cases, less informative responses despite the same methods and efforts being applied as in the North. Hopefully, the study will provide impetus for further research which might include, for example, stratification of a representative sample by sector, or analysis of skill–differentiation across different languages. There is certainly a need for a further national study to be centrally funded. The Peter Parker Report on Asian and African languages,[12] could provide the kind of industry–orientated model for evaluating specific foreign language issues facing the country in the future.

Objectives And Sample Selection

Contributors to the Part I surveys based on the North East questionnaire[13] follow broadly the same guidelines in their objectives and selection of data:

1   To provide an industrial and commercial profile of the region, or area, where the survey was carried out;
2   To evaluate the foreign language **needs** of firms in the sample according to:
    (a) their failure to increase trade significantly for lack of access to language facilities (Question 4)

(b) their reliance on outside translation/language agencies (Question 7)

3 To provide an indication of the pattern of foreign language need in terms of

(a) turnover (Question 10)

(b) industrial/commercial sector (Question 3)

(c) export–import profile (i.e. goods exported to non–English–speaking markets as a percentage of total sales) (Question 1)

4 To investigate companies' use of foreign languages

(a) by their own staff (Question 8)

(b) in transactions abroad with or without reliance on a local agent/interpreter (Question 3)

(c) a checklist of common business activities using languages (Question 6)

5 To evaluate the effect on the relative importance of different languages from patterns of projected trade (Question 5)

Addresses of firms in the mailshots were generally from the membership lists of Chambers of Commerce, Business Clubs or regional management/development centres without pre–selection according to size, sector, turnover or previous exporting success. Thus each regional sample covered a broad range of company–types, producing a reasonably representative cross–section of local industry. For the purposes of maintaining uniformity between samples the positive respondents were taken to be companies and firms which indicated some contact with foreign languages in the previous three years, however slight and in whatever way. Companies trading purely in the UK domestic market or in English–speaking countries like the USA or Ireland were excluded: i.e. companies indicating 'zero' in Q1(c), or in Q2(c),[14] which then crossed out Questions 3–8 as "Non–applicable" were left out of the final sample.[15] The percentage of these "rejects" ranged from 51.5% of the companies returning the questionnaire in East Anglia to 12.5% in the East Midlands of the companies returning the questionnaire).

The eight studies in Table 3 provide valuable early comparisons.[16] In terms of sample size and survey methodology, the present study bears some resemblance to the London Chamber of Commerce and Industry Survey of 593 member firms of its Overseas Divisions in 1972[17]. Both are questionnaire–based and provide evidence submitted by firms, rather than individuals responding in their own right. However, the focus of the LCCI study is more specific; it concentrates on the relative importance of different language activities for ten categories of personnel, without differentiation between languages.

By comparison, the York Report takes as its objective 'a pilot survey of British industry's manpower requirements in foreign languages'[18], having abandoned an earlier concept of attempting to measure language needs. The grounds for this change were (a) the improbability of industry being aware of its own foreign language needs and (b) the intangibility of need as a measurable concept.[19] This shift in emphasis led to a limited concentration on languages that *could be used* (i.e. French, German and Spanish), because the educational system provided them, and the job experience of languages graduates, i.e. specialist linguists. This thorny issue of the discrepancy between 'use' and 'need' is revisited and given some statistical credibility in the present analysis. Furthermore, the second emphasis on the role of *language graduates* in industry, given special prominence in earlier statistical surveys,[20] is here broadened to *languages* in industry.

As Liston and Reeves (1985)[21] have indicated, languages should be part of a broader framework of training for overseas trade. It is crucial for engineers, scientists and technicians to identify knowledge of a foreign language as an accessible and integral part of their range of useful, everyday skills. Moreover, companies are keenly aware that if they want to employ a graduate purely for his or, more probably, her language skills, their chances of finding someone with Chinese or Japanese, as opposed to French, for their newly developing Far Eastern market are about 50:1 against.

Since the eight studies in Table 3, several changes are apparent. Up to 1979 both the Barclays and the York studies painted a depressing picture: language competence was held in low esteem across much of British industry. From the BETRO Trust Survey onwards, the studies in 1979–1981 show relatively greater acknowledgement of the importance of languages, a point which has been clarified elsewhere.[27]

TABLE 3: SURVEYS OF BRITISH FIRMS USING FOREIGN LANGUAGES

Author or Short Title [22]	Year of Data [23]	Sample Size of Firms (N)
1 York Report [24]	1972	51
2 LCCI [25]	1972	593
3 Barclays Bank Int.	1978	120
4 BETRO Trust	1979	200
5 C Wilding	1979	49
6 R Savage	1980	(70) [26]
7 J Hurman	1981	121
8 Collinson *et al*	1981	76

However, marked reluctance of companies to employ individuals *equally for their linguistic skills*, as for their technical skills, remains the case. Despite the findings on employers' needs, it is still apparent that many firms remain unconvinced of the commercial advantages of taking on personnel with foreign language skills. Greatest employer recognition occurs, however, where foreign language skills are more clearly tangible, such as in the day–to–day handling of foreign correspondence. Both Morris[28] and Hurman[29] have produced evidence of greater job opportunity for bilingual (and trilingual) secretaries than for any other job category involving languages in industry.

One of the BETRO survey's key findings, nonetheless, is that the more successful export companies employ more linguists. Similarly, the York Report also found a correlation between companies' commitment to languages and export success, even though, at that time, it appeared the vast majority of employers remained unaware of it. Our findings substantiate this correlation, shedding particular light on the inter–relationship between company export profile, trade loss and changing patterns in the demand for languages.

Major Findings

One indication of the greater demand for languages in industry appears in the 10.6% increase in language use across matching samples of Northern industry between 1977–1984. In Chapter 1 it is estimated that as many as half the private companies in industry and commerce have used a foreign language for business in recent years, or employed someone to do so on their behalf. This upward trend is also apparent in the increasing number of LCCI entries for examinations in foreign languages for business, rising from 2023 in 1977 to 2603 in 1986.[30] The changing pattern of British trade is undoubtedly one important factor in this, but also the increasing predominance of French in the education system has also stimulated the learning of other languages beyond school.[31]

Evidence of additional language learning can also be seen in the range of foreign languages where firms in the survey claim in–house skills. Firstly, in Table 4 nearly 75% of all firms indicated that they had used one or more foreign languages in recent years. What is revealing is the broader diversification of languages represented here than is available at school. Nor can this discrepancy simply be attributed to the employment of native speakers, since this does not generally exceed 1–2% of cases. Clearly the need to develop skills in languages other than French for business purposes has led to noticeable levels of learning in German, Italian and other minority languages out of necessity. Significantly, three regions – Humberside, East Anglia and the SW – have used their employees more for German than for French.

There are other notable regional variations: speakers of Dutch, for example are more prevalent in regions with strong shipping and trade links with Holland; East Anglia, Humberside and North East England. French is more widely used than German in only five of the nine regions represented, emphasising the rough parity in business use between the two languages. However, these two are well ahead of the others; in–house Spanish and Italian skills are, on average, available to fewer than half the companies with French or German. No thorough evaluation of the level of ability across different languages has yet taken place and, perhaps not surprisingly, ability beyond a rusty 'O' level is rare in industry generally.

TABLE 4: IN-HOUSE COMPANY USE OF LANGUAGES

Region	% Sample claiming F.L. Skills	Languages used by firms' own staff (%)								
		F	G	S	I	Ar	J	Dut	R	Ch
N.E. (1)	75.5	62	49	22	18	6.5	2.5	7	2	2
N.E. (2)	64	50.5	44.5	18.5	11.5	2	2	5.5	0.5	0.5
Yorks	86	77	60.5	24.5	24.5	4.5	0	2.5	3.5	0.5
Hum	71	48	53.5	22	19	4	3	8	3	1.5
E.M.	46	61	61	20	19	5	2	2	5	1
Ox.	74	66	56	20	22	2	5.5	4.5	3.5	0
E.A.	83	69	73	25	17	8	10	12	5	3
S.E.	92	86.5	67	40.5	29	15.5	11.5	0	13.5	9.5
S.H.	85	72	60	21	15	8.5	4.5	2	0	2
S.W.	58	46	51.5	16	16	8	2.5	2.5	2.5	0
Average	73.5	64	57.5	23	19	6.5	4.5	4.5	4	2.5

Notes: 1 Percentages are based on the total sample of firms (N) in each region, as indicated in Table 2, col.5.

2 Percentages are rounded up to the nearest 0.5%.

3 Abbreviations for regions are given in the List of Common Abbreviations.

The parlous state of British companies' own in–house language abilities is also apparent from other studies. In the BETRO Trust Survey only 30% of the 200 export departments claim any linguistic ability and nearly one–third of 654 members of the Institute of Export questioned in a recent Gallup Poll had no knowledge of any foreign language.[32] Their range of language abilities is also in line with the pattern in our findings; French (54%), German (30%), Spanish (16%), Italian (8%), Arabic (4%) and Dutch (4%). Yet, according to the BETRO study, linguistic skills are more widespread in export departments than in any other area of industrial work, which makes the overall picture much gloomier.

One factor which companies claim deters them from recruiting linguists is the poor cost-effectiveness of employing a specialist if the frequency of foreign language use is low. Savage (1980)[33] found, for example, that only a quarter of the firms in his sample declared their contact with a foreign language was 'frequent', nearly half indicated 'seldom' and one-sixth said 'never'. This is similar to the finding in Chapter 1 where 26% of a sample of 614 Northern companies declared 'moderate' or 'extensive' use, while 33% indicated 'little' and 50.8% made 'nil' use of languages in 1984. In her article on Scottish companies, Margaret Ross reveals that 'frequent' use of Japanese occurs only with 3% of firms, yet Scottish exports to Japan run at £227 million p.a. – the fourth highest non-English speaking export outlet for Scottish goods after West Germany, France and the Netherlands.

The overwhelming message of all the studies in this volume is that British companies are losing valuable trading opportunities for lack of the right skills in the right languages, and many without realising it. The most disturbing evidence for this is the percentage of companies which admit they could have *significantly improved their trade performance* with access to certain foreign language facilities. Question 4 was deliberately worded to test whether evidence of a direct relationship between the role of foreign languages and trading performance existed in the mind of the respondent. The percentage of positive responses in each sample (see Table 5) was substantially higher than expected, ranging from 25% in the London Area (South East) to 60% in Yorkshire; i.e. an average of 44% across Britsh industry. This key finding of the study suggests that a substantial number of British companies now recognise that their lack of access to certain foreign languages and skills has lost them potential trade.

TABLE 5: FOREIGN LANGUAGES MOST NEEDED BY BRITISH REGIONS**

Region	% Sample in need	'N'	Languages needed (=Q4) (% of Firms)							
			F	G	Sp	It	Ar	J	R	Ch
NE (1)	54	168	26	27	15	8.5	13.5	5	3	2.5
NE (2)	44	151	28	22	13	5	12.5	4	3	2
Yorks	60	86	22	20	17.5	9.5	6	4.5	6	*
Hum	37	73	19	22	14	10	8	4	5.5	*
E.M.	41	105	23	17	14.5	5.5	5.5	8	5	4
Ox.	43	88	25	18	17	18	3.5	8	3.5	3.5
EA	44	59	27	15.5	13.5	7	10	10	3.5	7
S.E.	25	52	11.5	8	4	*	11.5	*	2	2
S.H.	47	47	28	23.5	19	6.5	15	*	2	*
S.W.	43	37	19	19	16	16	13.5	16	2.5	2.5
Average	44		23	19	13	9	10	6	4	2.5
Sussex	'Use'***	53	62.5	59	47	30	8	13	8	17
W.Scot	'Use'	160	44	38	35	12	12	3	2	*

*   Value is below 0.5% or negligible.

**   This table provides an overview of the relative need for different languages in response to Q4 on underperformance in trade for lack of foreign languages.

***   The Sussex and West of Scotland surveys provide comparable, though not matching, data on firms' *use* of languages.

The cross–regional perspective in Table 5 shows a remarkable degree of consistency in the relative importance of the languages needed. Three regional surveys put the need for German higher, or equal to, that for French (North East England, 1984; Humberside and the South West). Nonetheless, fewer than a quarter of the aggregate sample of firms in ten surveys needed French. The other three-quarters need mainly German, Spanish, Arabic, Italian, Japanese, Russian and Chinese. Other languages in lesser demand include Dutch, Portuguese, Swedish, Norwegian and Farsi. The obvious mismatch between industrial need and school provision is mentioned by several contributors, but, ironically, it is best summarised in the Department of Education and Science's own draft statement of policy, *Foreign Languages in the School Curriculum*, published in June 1986:

> "the current situation is clearly inappropriate to the needs of a modern trading nation ... Knowledge of a potential customer's language can be a deciding factor in securing and maintaining exports. A knowledge of competitors' languages can also confer an advantage." (para.35, p.12)

The evidence of need suggests that exporting firms in particular would benefit if the range of foreign languages and skills taught at school reflected recent patterns of international trade more closely. Despite an unused pool of teachers in Spanish, Italian and Russian, upon which schools could draw if the will were there, it seems that 'administrative convenience and self-perpetuating tradition' (para.33., p12) will continue to override the country's proven language needs until the circle can be broken. As there appears to be little action other than words to bring this about at present, the most enlightened companies will continue to buy in training programmes of the type described in Part II, while the majority will let trading opportunities slip them by. As Embleton points out in his article, 85% of the personnel surveyed at the ICI Chemicals and Polymers Wilton plant 'felt that language studies at school had not been relevant'. Although schools have been changing slowly with the introduction of new examination syllabuses (e.g. BTEC, TVEI, GCSE) and advent of the National Curriculum, it will take many years to dispel industry's view of language learning at school as largely inappropriate to the realities of international trade in the 80's.

Much of the perceived irrelevancy has to do with the mismatch between the traditional elements tested in a formal language examination, such as a prose translation, and the common business tasks requiring use of the foreign language. The most frequent use is, for example, 'reading letters or telex', i.e. simply understanding what the communication from abroad is about. Six of the samples in Table 6 indicate this activity as the most frequent; an average of 58%. In two other surveys, for which matching data are available, it comes second after 'wining and dining (social chat)' in Yorkshire and 'travelling' in the South West. The York Report[34] also ranks reading tasks as the most frequent, as do the other important surveys (i.e. the LCCI Survey's 'Basic responses'; Savage, 1980; Coutts, 1981).

The use of languages for 'travelling' is the second most common activity, averaging 52% over the samples. It is also given particular prominence in Embleton's ICI survey, where many of the respondents are involved in direct contact with ICI's subsidiary companies or customers abroad. But, as Wilding has pointed out,[35] 'travelling' can cover a very broad range of other activities; e.g. sales, visits to suppliers or agents, plant installation abroad and maintenance. Indeed, the tendency towards increased foreign business travel for international trade fairs, conferences and seminars, as well as overseas travel brought about by a tendency towards greater multinational company structure, is corroborated by the LCCI Survey of 350 German companies in 1982.[36]

The rank order of skill areas in our study largely confirm the pattern of the LCCI's earlier survey in the seventies, with only limited certain exceptions. First, the LCCI survey questionnaire contains substantially more categories of skill–area, such as 'conversation with one person', 'informal meeting 2–5 people', etc., which are simply omitted from our questionnaire for lack of space. However, neither our group, nor the LCCI, have investigated skill–use relative to *each* language. This problematic area is mentioned in Chapter 1, where 'use of the telephone' is placed lower down the list for Russian, due to the practical difficulties of telephoning to and from the USSR, whereas phone traffic between U.K. companies and the countries of the Common Market is substantial. Clearly the question of the extent to which language examination syllabuses should take account of differences in application between various languages needs further evaluation.

TABLE 6: MAJOR SKILL–AREAS WHERE FOREIGN LANGUAGES ARE USED

Regions	Skills/Activities (% of Firms)								
	Rlt	Trav	Ph	Wln	Chat	Rt	Wt	List	Gt
NE (1)	63.5	56.5	44.5	42	41	30	28	10	9
NE (2)	61.5	47.5	40.5	34	31	29	22	6	6
Hum	63	53.5	44	38.5	37	15	20.5	15	9.5
E.M.	62	51	52	51	29	33	27	6	8
OX.	63.5	55.5	59	43	37.5	38.5	29.5	16	17
E.A.	62	54	44	35	42	46	27	12	12
S.H.	49	61.5	44.5	40.5	42.5	42.5	36	4.5	6.5
S.W.	40.5	48.5	32.5	24.5	35	24.5	19	11	5.5
Average	58	53.5	45	38.5	36.5	34.5	26	10	9

N.B. The percentages are based on total samples (N)

Key: 1. Rlt: *reading letters/telex*; 2. Trav: *travelling abroad*; 3. Ph: *using the phone*; 4. Wln: *writing letters/notes*; 5. Chat: *social 'chat'*; 6. Rt: *reading letters/telex*; 7. Wt: *writing trade documents*; 8. List: *listening to talks*; 9. Gt: *giving talks/speeches*

Overall, 'speaking' and 'listening' are more useful than 'writing', which is used principally for correspondence and short notes. However, 'reading' needs to be given special attention in every business language syllabus, involving reading for detail, as well as for gist. In Research and Development departments, for example, accurate reading of patents, research articles and reports received in a foreign language can be vital to technological innovation. For example, in a survey of scientific publications worldwide,[37] although 45% were found to be in English, 55% were not. The implication for industry is obvious. There are major languages where a reading knowledge is particularly useful and British companies are missing out because their scientific personnel generally do not have the necessary foreign language access skills: namely, in German, French and Russian (comprising 35% altogether) and Japanese, Chinese, Arabic, Korean and Hindi (the other 20%). Every year thousands of potentially important patents (especially prior art) filed in Japan lie dormant. They remain linguistically inaccessible to most British companies and a 'blanket' translation is often too expensive a risk for the company to afford.[38] Unfortunately, a reading knowledge of German and Russian is a rare thing to find in scientists today.[39]

Particular value is also put on use of the foreign language in a social context by many respondents, particularly by those who travel and are involved in customer meetings and liaison. In rank order it averages fourth on our list, but the comments received suggest greater importance. For example, a few words of a difficult language used in a social setting can be an 'ice-breaker' and, as Anne Clark points out in her chapter, understanding informal conversations at conferences not only gives insight into attitudes, but also confidence to the listener.

Where business people have no knowledge of a particular language, or where they have too little to deal with foreign communications, patents or transactions, then reliance on outside agencies is essential, though sometimes costly and risky. On average, 60% of firms in Table 6 indicated having used a translation bureau. It is interesting to compare the rank order of languages where potential trading opportunities have been lost (Table 5) with demand for a translation agency (Table 7): here German assumes first place at 32%, ahead of French (29%), Arabic is very close behind Italian, while Russian and Chinese are roughly equal in seventh place. There are a number of reasons for these differences: firstly, most companies can rely more on their own personnel for French, whereas they usually have fewer who can read German. Secondly, Arabic is indecipherable for most British people and despatched to a bureau, whilst a French-speaker in a firm will normally try to process anything in Italian and save having the item translated.

Yet whilst the volume of Britain's visible trade is greater with Germany than with France, the Oxfordshire and Hampshire samples still place need for French translation ahead of German, while the South East and South West samples require equal levels of French and German. Regions in the North need more German than French, which may be due to the greater concentration of German-led engineering and metal manufacturing industries in those parts of the country.

TABLE 7: DEMAND FOR OUTSIDE TRANSLATION

Region	% Sample using trans bureaux	Languages bought in (Q7)(% of Firms)							
		G	F	Sp	Ar	It	Jap	R	Ch
NE (1)	71%	34	28	16	14	11	8	5.5	6.5
NE (2)	64%	37	29	14	12.5	11	5	4.5	4
Yorks	59%	31.5	25.5	22	8	15	8	7	*
Hum	47%	22	16.5	14	5.5	7	0	4	1.5
E.M.	57%	30	25	17	15	11	4	5	10
OX.	52%	24	27	14.5	8	10	5.5	5.5	3.5
E.A.	59%	34	27	17	12	14	10	7	8
S.E.	61.5%	32.5	32.5	23	27	7.5	9.5	7.5	11.5
S.H.	68%	40.5	42.5	19	13	15	4.5	*	4.5
S.W.	57%	32.5	32.5	16	16	19	5.5	2.5	*
Average	60%	32	29	17	13	12	6	5	5

Margaret Ross also indicates 'a substantial dependence on the services of agencies' in her study and highlights the appreciable element of cost for translation which many of the smaller companies cannot afford. Yet translation is misunderstood by a number of companies, as Noel Anderson observes in his article on the practical aspects of specialist translation. Often industry can also be inhibited by not distinguishing between professional translation agencies and 'cowboy outfits', particularly where there are different scales of costs. Dr Anderson's study sounds a note of caution to those companies who see no distinction between 'linguist' and 'translator', and who therefore undervalue the complex, but essential work of the technical translator, whilst not enquiring too closely into the professionalism of the outside translation agency.

Companies similarly rely too heavily on English–speaking local agents without enquiring too closely into their credentials. The commercial risks attached to excessive dependence on a local agent have also been highlighted in the York Report, as well as the Barclays Bank International and BETRO Surveys. It appears that few companies have heeded these warnings of the early seventies, nor taken account of what was described as 'the hidden cost (in terms of dearer imports or less competitive exports) of using agents overseas, part of whose function is to save British industry the inconvenience of mastering foreign languages' (York Report, p.11). In the BETRO Trust study 66% of the sample recognised the importance of speaking the local agent's language, especially in South America, France and Germany. Our study confirms not only the extent of the continuing reliance, but the dangers involved. Particular concern is apparent in the Northern Region where local agents are used by 50% of companies trading in Europe and 65% in the Middle and Far East. In the Yorkshire survey, 47 of the 86 companies use a local agent in foreign transactions; in East Anglia 20 companies out of 31 use their local agent for business abroad. The Oxfordshire survey noted, however, that the local agent was less prevalent in foreign-language only transactions, which is a positive sign of self-sufficiency. On the whole, as in the East Midlands report, at least half the companies surveyed use an agent for export deals.

Reliance on local interpreters can be even more dangerous than local agents, since the former have no vested self-interest in a profitable outcome to the transaction. One case, reported in *International Management*, concerned the speech of the leader of a Chinese delegation visiting North America, who described the newspaper hosting the banquet as 'one of the most influential, not only in North America, but in the world'. Instead, the interpreter came up with – "Thank you for lunch and we hope your newspaper will be successful one day."[40] Respondents to the Northern survey have also privately reported cases of vital commercial information either being omitted or deliberately glossed over by both interpreters and local agents, especially where the latter have no technical knowledge of the product under discussion.

As one might expect, however, English is used for most transactions abroad: it is overwhelmingly the language of importing, though not exclusively, as is pointed out, for example, in the Yorkshire, Humberside and Northern surveys. Of the 152 export transactions reported in the Humberside study 103 were in English, 29 in the local language and 19 in a mixture; figures which largely typify the other surveys. A mixture of languages was also found to be a relatively frequent occurrence (about 5–10% of occasions), emphasizing how transactions are the cross–roads of language and culture, where the purity of the mode of communication is subservient to the object of reaching a deal. The proportion of English–only transactions inevitably rises beyond the Near Continent: i.e. regions outside the linguistic scope of U.K. school provision. More research clearly needs to be done into the language of transaction in order to examine the exact consequences for U.K. trade of 'English–only' transactions.

One of the most important findings of the study is the link between company profile and language need. Certain sectors of industry appear to be in greater need than others. This is in line with Savage's finding (1980: 4–6) which relates frequency of language use to industrial category. However, as Hagen (1986:25–6) has shown for German in the North East, the pattern of *use* may not necessarily correspond to pattern of *need*. In Professor Cobb's article on the South East, the most bouyant export industries, i.e. chemicals, aircraft, information systems, software, non–ferrous metals and electronics, make up a far smaller share of the positive respondents, than companies in sectors with a poorer ratio of exports to domestic sales, such as mechanical, instrument and precision engineering.

It is manufacturing in general, and the engineering sectors in particular, especially mechanical, which appear to be in greatest need of language support across the country, though there are certain predictable regional variations, such as the needs of the textile industry in Yorkshire. Notably, the North–South divide is less prominent than this sectoral distinction. On the other hand, the smaller size of sample in the South may reflect less concern about languages, i.e. where there is greater prosperity, than in more economically depressed areas of Northern Britain. By comparison, the service sector is better represented in the East Anglian sample, comprising over 30% of the total, than in any other regional survey. Despite this, demand is still particularly high in the electronics, precision and mechanical engineering sectors within that region.

Any inconsistencies in the overall picture of company practice also have to do with the *culture and attitudes* prevailing in a particular firm rather than with external features, like company type or product. As

Kate Chambers and Professor Chris Cobb show in their analyses of good company practice, there can be wide variation in approach to international business, depending on the type of management. For example, in Chambers' survey of West Yorkshire polyglot textile firms, one manager whose firm covered five languages and exported 95% of its goods was still prepared to admit his company had lost opportunities for lack of the right languages. In fact, it seems to be a general rule that those who argue most vehemently that there is little need to learn foreign languages are almost without exception the ones who have not done so themselves and who remain unaware of the advantages. Where top management includes convinced linguists, such as Peter Blackburn in Rowntree Mackintosh plc, there is a greater chance that international awareness, including a re-evaluation of the importance of speaking languages, will permeate to all levels of the company.

It is usually firms smaller than Rowntree Mackintosh and ICI, however, which face the most acute language difficulties. This is apparent across all regions, for example, in the correlation between a company's annual turnover and its need for foreign languages . In the South East the firms in need are described as 'smaller'; in the North East they are mostly within an annual turnover band of between half a million and £20 million; in Oxfordshire two-thirds of the firms have a turnover less than £5 million. The relationship between company size and language problems referred to in an earlier study[41] is given strong numerical credibility in this collection.

Data on company export activity in non-English-speaking markets provide a further indicator of potential foreign language demand. There appears to be a consistent threshold of sales to non-English-speaking markets as a percentage of total sales turnover, beyond which concern about languages is generally not reported. For example, two-thirds of companies responding positively in the South West survey exported under 20% of their turnover to non-English-speaking countries; in Oxfordshire 87% exported under 40% of turnover; in the East Midlands 64% exported under 25% of turnover; in Yorkshire the percentage was 86% for under 50% of sales turnover. The pattern is further confirmed in Table 12 of the Northern study in Chapter 1 where over 70% of the companies with a declared need exported less than 30% of their goods to non-English-speaking countries and, as might be expected, half this sample of 'underperformers' sold less than 10% of their goods to these markets. The majority of companies which responded to the survey have a greater volume of sales in the U.K. domestic market than in non–English–speaking countries. It is principally when companies are in the initial stages of exporting to non–English–speaking countries, particularly when their sales to these markets are below 20% of total sales that awareness of a languages gap most develops.

Regrettably, it is often only the companies with a turnover of over £100 million sales – and an internationally–oriented management – which opt for a language training programme in response to the perceived gap. Companies of this size are also more keenly aware of the mismatch between the language skills available to them in their workforce, and the demands of the market. By comparison, most smaller firms will either 'get by with English' in the new market or abandon the export opportunity altogether on the grounds of difficulty of market penetration. Ironically, this latter scenario seems to apply to France in particular, despite the predominance of French in the schools. For example, in 1979 the British Chamber of Commerce in France issued a rare policy statement[42] on Britain's lost export opportunities in France, having identified in an earlier report one of the causes as the lack of people in British export departments who were able to understand French import procedures and use French[43].

The route to successful trading lies in combining knowledge of the business practice, culture and language of the foreign market. The common denominator is, however, the language. One company reported to the Northern Survey that it had had particular difficulty during the purchase of a French factory with the *Comité d'entreprise*, whose function had not been fully appreciated by the British negotiators. Not only was it **not** deemed necessary to communicate with it in French but non–French speakers had falsely believed its function was unimportant; a committee supporting *'enterprise' (sic)*. The French work force was angered and shocked by this display of ignorance by the British management and the resulting bad blood almost jeopardised the entire negotiations.

Introduction

The value of a cultural input into language training programmes is brought out in Part II. Robert Taylor of IC Ltd refers to the need to include culture and protocol information, while Anne Clark emphasises the value of including current German newspaper articles in a course for a Senior Manager who has to interact socially with West Germans at a high level.

Yet one valuable additional function of language training programmes is to *change the culture* of the British company by promoting internationalism amongst its own employees. As Doug Embleton argues in his article on ICI's Wilton plant, the crucial aim is to create *language awareness* throughout the company. Language awareness, when achieved through learning another language, leads logically to the perception that those who speak differently also have a different order of preferences and priorities in the way they do business. Changing people's attitudes to languages in Britain does not, however, have history on its side. It may take a generation for Britain first to adjust its own attitudes and then develop new aptitudes.

For international companies like Rowntree Mackintosh, ICI and Peugeot Talbot, the need to train personnel in foreign languages is not a nicety, but an *economic necessity*. Peter Blackburn puts it simply as, 'no language, no business'. Many examples of concrete situations where a foreign language is used are given in Part II, together with quotations from business people who testify to the advantages of learning a language. In general, foreign–language users have gained more respect abroad; been more efficient in communicating; felt at ease; made closer friendships; found out vital information from asides while socialising; responded quickly to urgent 'phone and telex messages; reduced their company's reliance on agents; handled foreign acquisitions more sensitively; gained the upper hand in transactions; saved unnecessary expenditure on translators and interpreters; done their own market research; solved problems immediately by talking directly to shopfloor workers; travelled more comfortably; made a greater impression at conferences; in short, improved not only their company's and their own image abroad, but, more significantly, contributed immeasurably to their company's international business success.

Introduction

Part II provides examples of successful training models and approaches which offer complementary solutions to many companies' export needs. Robert Taylor's description of his company's approach to analysing a firm's language needs and setting up corresponding in-company programmes provides a valuable structural overview of all the stages and sub-stages involved in the Language Audit. By contrast, Anne Clark's case studies complement Robert Taylor's analytical survey by introducing specific profiles of learners, emphasising the diversity and urgency of demand apparent in large companies. Above all, it is the *relevance* of the materials and the language to the specific purpose which counts.

Marion Smart's study of language training in Peugeot Talbot is distinctive by being wholly concerned with one language, French, while IC Ltd and Halton College offer packages across all languages. This concentration on one language means that statistics for learning rates in French can be given with some degree of accuracy on the basis of many years' experience. Furthermore, the motivation amongst the work force for learning French in a French-controlled car plant in Coventry could not be higher. This perhaps explains why Marion Smart's unit has achieved remarkable success with over 1,500 (out of a workforce of 4000) employees having received training in French over seven years. However, even for highly motivated learners, it is clear from all our studies that mature, busy people who lack linguistic grounding from their schooldays, or who have never learnt a foreign language early on, face a major disadvantage in later life. As Marion Smart admits, mature students starting a language from scratch 'acquire only a thin veneer'. Language learning is only really successful over a long period. Thus, it is understandable why major companies combine Crash Courses with the regular, weekly drip-feed approach; i.e. what Doug Embleton terms 'training for stock'. The 'Crash Course', or short intensive tuition, survives as a last resort for an emergency, where an employee needs 'survival language' for the immediate future. It remains, nonetheless, a poor substitute for the language-learning missing from the school curriculum.

The fact that a number of large companies have adopted a languages policy, involving a regular language-learning scheme, suggests a long-term commitment to international markets, particularly the EEC.

They recognise the need, for example, of being able to compete with German companies in West Germany on equal terms, which means eliminating any linguistic disadvantage. As 1992 approaches, moreover, British companies will find they will have more access to trained and skilled European personnel from the Continent who can offer competence in several languages in addition to their professional qualifications. Unless there is a fundamental change in policy and national attitudes, Britons who speak only English could soon miss out on the new era of cross-European recruitment policies in major companies.

The Future

The most striking feature of international trade is not so much the widespread use of English as the evident bi-lingualism and, frequently, tri-lingualism of the leading participants. The languages gap in British industry remains largely unfilled except, perhaps, for attempts by some companies at grafting relevant language and skills on the workforce late in life in response to immediate need. In the longer term, however, the nation's serious linguistic deficiencies can only be corrected by a radically new approach to languages in the schools and a widespread change in popular attitudes. Only when bi-lingualism is perceived as *more attractive* in English culture than mono-lingualism will a long-lasting solution be in the making.

Outside events are, however, bringing the prospect of such a change in attitudes into the realms of possibility. With the entry into force of the Single European Act in 1992 and the creation of an "area without frontiers"[44], freedom of movement and the lifting of barriers will tend to highlight inadequacies of people who speak one language and slowly disenfranchise them culturally within European society. As British companies increasingly appreciate the value of recruiting multi-lingual personnel in penetrating different European markets, so public perceptions will radically alter. Indeed, the widespread recruitment of Continental Europeans for their 'better commercial training' (and superior knowledge of languages), in preference to the British, is not without historical precedent. The situation in 1898 was surprisingly similar:

Introduction

"British business was apparently not training up a class of men from which to recruit sufficient first-class commercial travellers; indeed, many of the representatives employed by British firms were of necessity Germans."[45]

The foundations for later language training must be laid in the schools. Apart from teaching the appropriate language skills, the role of British education is crucial in developing a more general awareness of international culture and, in particular, more positive language-learning habits. In part, the development of languages in this country has been seriously curtailed by their designation as an Arts subject within the curriculum, rather than as a medium of expression applicable equally to science and technology as to literature and the Humanities. Industry's need for foreign languages has also been aggravated by the disproportionate drop-out of boys from the modern language option and the excessive preoccupation with French[46] to the detriment of all other languages in the school curriculum. The illogicality of Britain's languages policy is even more apparent when we examine the situation in other countries like France, for example,[47] or Sweden, which was offering 82 foreign languages in the seventies![48].

Most industrialists and business people argue that they expect the school system to achieve three objectives:

- to teach every child a basic knowledge of at least one foreign language (not always French) and how to use it for practical, useful purposes;

- to ensure that languages are started early and not quickly dropped, especially by boys doing sciences;

- to ensure a greater diversification of languages and skills, which are more in tune with the needs of international trade in the 90s.

Whilst it may be unrealistic to teach *all languages* at school, it is vital to develop both the capacity to learn languages, as well as an openness to other cultures, in the nation's schoolchildren. Firstly, learning a language at school provides the individual with a foundation for more effective learning of other languages later in life; one language obviously acts as a bridge to another. Secondly, since companies are broadly consistent in their projection of the future pattern of international trade, educational planners should not shy away from taking bold steps now on the basis of forecast future needs. For example, our findings show that the broad direction of British trade is still increasingly towards Western Europe (i.e. particularly Germany and France), then the Middle East (Arabic), the Far East (Japanese, Chinese) and Latin America (Spanish and Brazilian Portuguese). A country of Britain's size, so dependent on foreign trade, should offer all these core languages and cultures somewhere in the school curriculum, thus ensuring a pool of individuals with a diverse enough range of languages and a developed sense of other cultures, on whom the country can draw in future. Each child should learn two languages and be exposed to 'taster' courses in others. Finally, where existing provision in other languages has been allowed to run down, i.e. in Russian and Italian, what remains clearly has to be bolstered. Both the USSR and Italy are valuable markets where the core languages cannot be used directly; it is a common fallacy that German is adequate for trading with the USSR and French suffices in Italy.

Apart from tangible evidence of the link between trade performance and languages cited here and elsewhere (Reeves, 1985; Skapinker, 1986; Bungay, 1986; Statham, 1981), it is what is left unsaid, i.e. the hidden cost, that is most disturbing. For obvious reasons, companies are usually unwilling to divulge examples of their own errors and failings, and far less able to cost them in terms of the potential lost trade. In many cases, business people remain blindly unaware of the consequences of their own language failings, while others can recall the concrete advantages they have had from knowing the local language. One respondent from the North of England, for example, overheard a vital conversation in German between a foreign buyer and a rival sales rep, whilst waiting in the next room. The information she gleaned then enabled her to win the business. On the other hand, another respondent declared he had travelled widely in Germany and been 'successful' with *only* English. Another respondent felt it was 'deceitful' to listen in to people's private business discussions abroad, though he did not speak a foreign language himself. However, many who do not speak a foreign language still recognise the inestimable value of knowing one, especially when establishing personal relations.

Industry also loses out on information which goes unread, simply because few have a reading knowledge of the particular foreign language and even fewer in languages other than French. More disturbing again is the danger, and widespread use, of non-specialists left to handle complex information in a foreign language. In some parts of industry there is even ignorance about the differences between foreign languages; employees with knowledge of *one* foreign language are expected to handle *all* foreign language communications. Companies have also sent information in Spanish to Brazil and in German to the USSR, without realising the effect of their error. Reasons for the consequent lack of response are then put down to rejection of the *product*, rather than the *language of presentation*.

In the more forward-looking parts of British industry, such as ICI or Rowntree Mackintosh, major strides have already been made to create the international awareness and linguistic capability necessary for the world market of the 90s. In the case of ICI's Chemicals and Polymers Ltd. at Wilton, this has been most noticeable in the recent rapid growth in the translation of sales and product literature into the customer's language, rising from 16, in 1979 to 129 in 1987[49]. This policy of adopting the customer's language comes from a company which consistently gathers its own market intelligence (brochures) abroad and clearly recognises the commercial advantages. Terry Cox, a Business Marketing Manager at ICI Chemicals and Polymers Ltd., recently summed up his own perception of the situation in industry:

> "Knowing a foreign language gives you an added dimension,
> an unquantifiable commercial edge or advantage. Languages
> are used increasingly, *pro rata* with business growth, and
> there's only an element of truth in the belief that English is
> the language of world business."
> (Interview with Editor, 19.11.87)

The message of the studies in this book is both disconcerting and challenging. The scale of the problem facing commerce and industry in Britain is set out with numerical precision. Training solutions and models provide only one answer to the country's languages gap; there has to be a radical change in attitude. The changing pattern of international trade and the impact of 1992 provide both the occasion and opportunity for a radical re-think and a review of provision in languages. If the challenge to change is taken up, the cultural and trade benefits to the British people promise to be of inestimable value. If not, the hidden cost to industry will continue rising, Britain will remain Anglocentric and its people culturally marginalised in an increasingly multilinguistic and multicultural world.

References And Notes

1. The term 'company' is used for terminological convenience and includes firms which are not incorporated, as well as branch plants which are autonomous and separately located from the company HQ.

2. W.S.H. Gaskell (1897) *Our trade in the World in Relation to Foreign Competition, 1885–1895*. Quoted in R.J.S. Hoffman *Great Britain and the German Trade Rivalry 1875–1914*, New York: Garland 1983, p.88

3. *European Survey 1979*. The Council of British Chambers of Commerce in Europe, June 1979.

4. N. Reeves (1985) Education for Exporting Capability – Languages and Market Penetration, *The Incorporated Linguist*, 24, No.3/4, pp.147–153.

5. *Ibid.*, p.149.

6. *Ibid.*, p.150.

7. *Ibid.*, p.149. Quoted from the 'Second Report from the Trade and Industry committee. Session 1983–84. The Growth in the Imbalance of Trade in Manufactured Goods between the U.K. and Existing and Prospective Members of the EEC'. HMSO, London 1985.

8. Further clarification is given by authors in their separate acknowledgements.

9. S. Hagen, Trading in Other Tongues, *T.H.E.S.*, 10/5/85.

10. J.W. Coutts, A Pilot Investigation into the Foreign Language Needs of International Trade. Unpublished M.A. Dissertation, London University, 1981, p.39.

11. The 'others' use a different questionnaire, though the data are comparable.

12. *Speaking for the Future: A Review of the Requirements of Diplomacy and Commerce for Asian and African Languages and Area Studies.* A report submitted by Sir Peter Parker MVO to the University Grants Committee, 1985.

13. See Appendix 1.

14. *Ibid.*

15. The percentages in the tables of each survey are based on this sample of foreign–language–using companies (N) given in column 5 in Table 2, unless otherwise indicated by authors.

16. For an overview of surveys, see Wilding, C. (1980) *Languages, Education and Industry. A Summary of Reports and Conferences,* Aston University; or, more recently, Reeves, N. (1985) and Hantrais, L. (1985) *Using Languages in a Career,* Aston: AMLC., pp.8–28.

17. *The Non–Specialist Use of Foreign Languages in Industry and Commerce,* LCCI Examinations Board, Revised Ed., 1985.

18. Emmans *et al* (1974), p.9.

19. *Ibid.*

20. L. Hantrais, *Using Languages in a Career,* Aston: AMLC, 1985, pp.8–27.

21. D. Liston and N. Reeves (1985) *Business Studies, Languages and Overseas Trade: A Study of Education and Training.*

22. Full publication details are given in the Bibliography.

23. The year of data collection normally precedes year of publication.

24. This sample is of employers from Section 5 of the York Report and covers 611 employees in the 51 companies.

25. LCCI Examinations Board (1985) *The Non–Specialist Use of Foreign Languages in Industry and Commerce.*

26. The total sample (N) does not appear in the publication and is estimated.

27. See, for example, Hantrais (1985) p.28.

28. Cynthia J. Morris: Are Modern Languages of Any Use? A Limited Survey of Job Opportunities for Modern Linguists. *Modern Languages* Vol.LXI No.3 Sept 1980 pp 109–112. In 720 job advertisements requesting foreign language skills, $50^1/_2\%$ were for bi- or tri–lingual secretaries.

29. John D. Hurman: Modern Linguists: Industrial demand and school supply –a survey and a proposal; *Modern Languages* Vol.LXIII No.1 March 1982 pp44–48.

30. M. Dixon: As it is spoken, *Financial Times,* 21/2/87 p.XV.

31. One specific example of this is the increase in registrations at Newcastle Polytechnic's open–access language laboratory from 251 in 1980/1 to 423 in 1985/6. 30% of the latter were 'vocational–users'.

32. D. Liston and N. Reeves (1985) p.121.

33. R.F. Savage (1980) Modern Languages in Education and Industry in Staffordshire. Staffordshire County Council, p4–6.

34. Emmans *et al.,* (1974) p.40.

35. C. Wilding (1979/80) Unpublished Survey through the Careers

Office of the University of Aston in Birmingham.

36. LCCI Survey, p.30.

37. R. Quirk: English is not Enough. *THES*, 11/12/87 p.13.

38. S. Hagen (1988) *Forthcoming*.

39. In some cases British universities, and polytechnics are partly to blame for not recognising and resourcing the servicing role of Modern Language departments on science, engineering and business courses especially for languages other than French.

40. M. Skapinker: Why speaking English is no longer enough. *International Management*, November 1986, p.40.

41. C. Wilding (1980) *Languages, Education and Industry*, p.16.

42. *A Policy Statement:* the British Chamber of Commerce France, Autumn 1979.

43. Export attitudes in the United Kingdom: an enquiry conducted by the British Chamber of Commerce France, June 1979. For an analysis, see C. Wilding, (1980), p.19.

44. *Europe, Our Future, 1992: A European Areas without Frontiers* (June 1987) Commission of the European Communities.

45. RJS Hoffman, (1983), p88.

46. In approximate terms, there have been five times as many pupils taking CSE French as German; three times as many doing GSE 'O' level in French as German; twice as many university students read French as German.

47. Only 2% of British pupils learn German compared with 19% of all pupils in France who learn German. There are also almost twice as many German teachers in France than in the U.K. It seems strange that the French, whose first foreign language is now English, devote

substantially more resources to German, the second language in their schools, than the British do, when German is the *first* language of industry in some British regions.

48. R. Savage, (1980) Quoted on the inside cover.

49. Interview between D. Embleton and the Editor on 7/1/88 at Wilton. The 129 items added up to approximately 2,000 pages.

– PART I –
SURVEYS

Chapter 1

THE FOREIGN LANGUAGE DEMANDS OF INDUSTRY AND COMMERCE IN THE NORTHERN REGION OF ENGLAND
Stephen Hagen

The Regional Context

The Northern Region of England is a region which provides a particularly apt model for studying the foreign language needs of industry. It has a clear regional identity, comprising North East England (Northumberland, Co. Durham, Cleveland) and Cumbria; it has a population of nearly three million, half of whom live along the 50-mile stretch between Newcastle upon Tyne and Middlesbrough; it has a strong industrial tradition in mechanical and electrical engineering and 28% of the working population are still employed in manufacturing.

At a glance, the region seems to epitomise many of the industrial ills besetting the country: it has one of the worst unemployment rates of any UK region, with the biggest job losses – in the metal goods, engineering and vehicle sector – recently up to 10,000 per annum. Its manufacturing sector has been subject to high levels of extra-regional acquisition; 80% of plants are now controlled by companies with headquarters outside the region. Moreover, the North's GDP places it in the bottom quarter of European regions. Yet, on the other hand, the region is showing strong signs of industrial and commercial regeneration: some 15 Japanese manufacturing and hi-tech companies have recently moved into the region to join the 160 American and European companies already established. Alongside the declining industries of coal mining and shipbuilding stand giants of the chemical and petrochemical industry, such as ICI Chemicals and Polymers Ltd. on Tees-side, well-established companies of the pharmaceutical industry (eg Bristol-Myers, Glaxo), clothing manufacturers (eg Burberry's) and electronics companies (eg Plessey, NEI Electronics, Elmwood Sensors), which maintain a strong profitable presence and investment in the region.

Fortunately, the prospects for the region are not as bleak today as they have been for a number of years. There has been a considerable decrease in the unemployed/vacancy ratio, which has fallen below 20 for the first time in the 1980s; the North is also sharing in the nationwide growth of service employment, evidenced, for example, in the upsurge of the retail sector in enterprising and imaginative developments like the Metro Centre in Gateshead. On the other hand, the North's service sector growth cannot replace the volume of manufacturing jobs lost and workers in the North are still more likely to be made redundant than those in Great Britain as a whole.

The North has traditionally depended upon the competitiveness of its products in the world market and if its shrinking manufacturing sector is to survive, it has to maintain a market share in European countries like France and West Germany with their larger domestic markets. In the analysis of returns from a broad cross-section of companies sampled over ten years (1977–1986), it seems to be the case that the growing Europeanisation (if not internationalisation) of local companies has brought with it a sharper awareness of the commercial advantages of speaking the customer's language.

The use of foreign languages across virtually the same sample of approximately 600 companies examined first in 1977 and again in 1984 showed an increase of 10.6% and the two later studies of 1984 and 1985 showed an identifiable, but unsatisfied, need for language skills which confirmed the upward trend. In order to assess the nature of this change, and its consequences for future provision of language skills, it became essential to monitor industry's needs more systematically by on-going surveys.

Survey Objectives, Methods And Chronology

The 'Foreign Language Use in Northern Commerce and Industry' study (or 'FLUNCI') was initiated in 1984 with six broad objectives in mind:

- to establish the relative importance and extent of use of foreign languages across a broad cross-section of Northern companies;

- to measure the unsatisfied *need* for languages amongst companies, as evidenced in (a) companies' own admission of

lost trading opportunities and (b) reliance upon outside
agencies for language skills;

–   to establish the degree of in–house language competence
claimed across companies;

–   to investigate the language of negotiation in recent trade
deals and the use of local agents/interpreters abroad;

–   to examine the relationship between export performance,
company turnover and the foreign language profile of
companies;

–   to gain a perspective on where future trade was most likely to
occur and hence which languages would be needed.

To achieve the first objective, it has been possible to draw upon
unpublished data from four earlier questionnaire–based surveys carried
out between 1977 and 1984.

**TABLE 1:   SURVEYS OF NORTHERN COMMERCE AND
INDUSTRY   1977–1984** [1]

Survey No	Year	Sample Size (Respondents)	% Respondents using For. Langs.	Actual No. of Lang. Users
1	1977 (i)	580	38.6	224
2	1977 (ii)	34*	100	34
3	1981	94	80.9	76
4	1984	614	49.2	302
	TOTAL	1,322	TOTAL	636

* Known exporters only

TABLE 2: SURVEYS OF NORTHERN COMMERCE AND INDUSTRY ('FLUNCI') 1984–1986[2]

Survey No	Year	Sample Size (Respondents)	% Respondents using For. Langs.	Actual No. of Lang. Users
5	1984	241	69.7	168
6	1985	193*	78.2	151
7	1985/6	118	60.2**	71**
TOTAL		552	TOTAL	390

* Known exporters only

** Only potential users of Middle Eastern/Oriental languages selected

When the earlier surveys are taken alongside the three 'FLUNCI' studies 1984–1986 in Table 2, the Northern Region has the accolade of being more extensively studied for its industrial and business use of languages than any other British region. Whilst each of the earlier surveys had its own objectives not directly connected with later ones, each has produced complementary data which permit cross–checks between samples over a ten–year period. A virtually complete picture of the industrial application of languages emerges against the changing pattern of regional development. Taken overall, the Northern Regional study involves 1,832 responses, of which 1,026 state their firms use foreign languages. By taking samples of hundreds rather than tens, it has been possible to reduce sampling error relative to previous surveys in this field. Moreover, the broad similarity of the findings across these different surveys suggests that there is a regular pattern of foreign language use and need amongst Northern companies.

Which Language?

Over the ten year period of the study the relative frequency of use of foreign languages across Northern industry and commerce has remained remarkably consistent. Trends apparent in early surveys have been confirmed in later ones. Overall the demand is for (1) German, (2) French, (3) Spanish, (4) Italian and Arabic.

Apart from plotting the findings on the relative importance of languages in use over ten years, other issues are worth investigating, such as the distinction between language *use* and language *need* and the growing importance of the languages of the Middle and Far East.

Early Surveys

As early as 1977 a sample of 34 known language users confirmed German to be a short head in front of French: German 76.5%; French 73.5%; Spanish 32.4%; Italian 29.4%; Arabic, Russian 8.8%; Turkish 5.9%; Dutch and Japanese 2.9%. However, the main emphasis of the survey was on trying to determine the main skills or disciplines of language users on the assumption, based on a general finding that languages are principally seen as an ancillary skill. The attempt to obtain a quantified response to the departments where languages were most used produced: 'sales and admin' 38%; 'marketing/export' 29%; 'engineering' 26.5%; 'secretarial' 9%. Unfortunately, no attempt to differentiate between languages was carried out at that stage.

The polytechnic's regular survey of local industry in the Northern Region covers approximately 600 medium–sized to large companies (with over 50 employees). What is significant here is not only the massive sample size but the random effect of the sampling for language users. Since the survey covers all types of commercial and industrial companies across the industrial classification list, it gives us a highly representative cross–section of companies in the North East and Cumbria, from which we can establish an overall pattern of language use for given languages across most Northern industries.

Between the two large–scale surveys of 1977 and 1984 there was an increase of 10.6% in the number of companies claiming to use languages for business; ie rising from 38.62% in 1977 to 49.2% in 1984 (where N = 580 and 614 respectively). Of the total number of these declared language users 143 companies use German and 132 French. If, however, we compute German users as a percentage of the total sample of 614 (see Fig. 1), including companies not using any foreign languages, we may extrapolate that 23.3%, ie nearly a quarter, of all types of medium–sized to large companies in the Northern Region may be using German and 21.5% French, or employing others to do so on their behalf. This is, of course, only a hypothesis, but the resulting pattern produces what is possibly more representative of the true picture than one offered by the conventional language surveys of known users.

FIG. 1:   RANK ORDER OF LANGUAGES IN USE (1984)
           (N = 614)

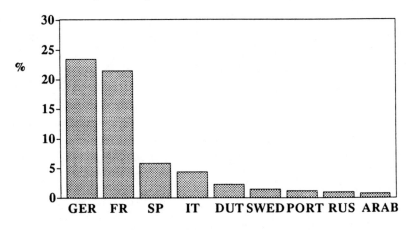

The figures would be less meaningful, however, if no account were taken of the *extent* of use. Companies were also asked to indicate their use of foreign languages on a scale ranging from 'nil' to 'extensive':

1977 SAMPLE (N = 580)		1984 SAMPLE (N = 614)	
'nil'	61.4%	'nil'	50.8%
'some'	11%		
'v. little'	10%	'little'	33%
'limited'	8%		
'exports only'	3.5%	'moderate'	14%
'extensive'	4%	'extensive'	2%

Given that the sample includes all types of company, many of which have no interest in languages (eg retailers), it is highly significant that 302 companies, nearly half the sample in 1984, needed to use a foreign language at some point in recent years. Moreover, the combined total for 'moderate' and 'extensive' in 1984 was 16%, suggesting that there has been approximately a 12% increase in 'moderate to extensive' use over the seven–year period.

'Use' or 'Need'?

Whereas the surveys in 1977 (i) and 1984 focus on 'use' the FLUNCI study is primarily concerned with 'need'. Planned in three stages over three years (1984 – 1986), the first two surveys involved, firstly, a random sample of 241 companies and organisations (1984) and, secondly, a selected sample of 151 likely exporters (1985). The third stage (1985/6) concentrated on the specific need for non–European languages in deep–sea trade – a rapidly increasing phenomenon with the growing importance of the Far East and S.E. Asia.

In 1984 168 companies out of 241 respondents (69.7%) indicated they were foreign language users. Given that the BOTB estimates that there are some 900 established companies exporting from the region, we may extrapolate that our sample could be as high as 20% of the absolute number, so that the true 'needs' of the region may be five times greater than our findings in numerical terms. Firstly, the critical regional deficiency in foreign languages is clear from the 54% of survey respondents in 1984 who indicated that they could have *significantly improved their trade performance* with access to foreign languages. In numerical terms 91 Northern companies out of 168 admitted they underperformed for lack of access to foreign language facilities. If we multiply our sample by five to give us an approximate absolute total of companies with language needs in the region, then a staggering 455 companies could be under–achieving, leading to lost orders for the region. As we see in Fig.2. German is the language most *needed*, as well as the most *used*.

FIG. 2:   'FLUNCI' SURVEY (1984) NEEDS ANALYSIS (N=168)

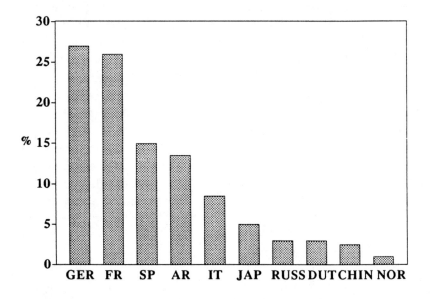

Significantly, Arabic is fourth on the list, very close behind Spanish, suggesting that a major re-think of foreign language provision would be entirely justified in the Northern Region if vocational-need criteria were applied to language classes in schools, colleges and training centres. An important cross-check is provided by evidence of reliance on outside language agencies to satisfy companies' needs. In this case the order G.Fr.Sp.Ar. was confirmed, though the recourse to agencies for German was significantly greater than for French (34% and 28% respectively). Spanish was 16% and Arabic was again close behind with 14% (where N=168). The need for German outstripping French is also apparent from a survey of freelance linguists and translators in 1981 (Survey 3 in Table 1) who indicated the principal languages in demand were German 35.9%, French 30.8%, Spanish 17.9% and Italian 5.1% (Collinson *et al.*, 1981: 75).

In the 1985 sample, fewer companies (44%) indicated lost trading opportunities for lack of languages. But, given the type of sample – namely, exporters, a figure of over 40% is no less distrubing. Amongst these, the rank order of languages **needed** was: (N = 151)

1. French (28%)   4. Arabic (12%)   7. Russian (3%)
2. German (22%)   5. Italian (5%)   7. Norwegian (3%)
3. Spanish (13%) 6. Japanese (4%) 9. Chinese (2%)

Two points can be made about these figures: firstly, German remained most in demand if we take into account use of translation agencies (G–37%; F– 29%; Sp–14%; Arabic–12%; Italian–11%; Japanese–5%; Russian–4%; where N = 151). Secondly, demand for French can be higher than for German because many companies recognise that France is inaccessible without French, whereas in Germany there is a greater willingness to use English. Not surprisingly, the need for French also reflects a mismatch between school French and the needs of business; in 1984 61% of the firms who claimed in–house skills in French also claimed to have lost opportunities for lack of French, and a similar figure (55%) was also evident in 1985. Despite the low level of French skills in industry, even business people with a smattering of the language have found it useful, both in Europe and overseas.

Which Non–European Language?

The four non–European languages with the most importance for the region's trading performance are: Arabic, Japanese, Chinese (mainly Mandarin) and Korean. Arabic is in some ways the region's forgotten fourth language, little used, only 2% in 1984, but very much more in need – 13.5% in 1984 and 12.5% in 1985. The demand is similarly confirmed by the number of companies relying on outside translation services for it – 20% and 12% in 1984 and 1985 respectively. In response to a request from Sir Peter Parker for specific data on the precise industrial needs in the region for African and Oriental languages in Northern industry, a more sharply focussed study carried out between October 1985 and January 1986 produced the findings in Table 3, based on responses to the questionnaire in Appendix 2:

TABLE 3:   THE 1985/6 'FLUNCI' SURVEY OF COMPANIES
           USING NON-EUROPEAN LANGUAGES FOR
           TRADE (N = 73)

Non-Eur. Language	% Firms using Lang	% Firms using own staff	% Firms using Lang Agency	% Firms using Local Agent	% Firms needing Lang*
Arabic**	50.7	8.2	31.5	19.2	26.0
Chinese	30.1	4.1	19.2	17.8	31.5
Japanese	20.5	1.4	9.6	12.3	23.3
Korean	12.3	0	2.7	6.8	6.8
Farsi	4.1	1.4	2.7	1.4	1.4

NB   *This figure is for companies who could increase, or could have
       increased, trade with access to skills in the language. The
       positive response rate to the question was 54.8%; and only
       28.2% indicated categorically they could not have increased
       trade, 13.7% gave a nil response and 2.7% said 'possibly'.

**   Arabic predominates over the other non-European languages
       except in the one category of 'need', where Chinese is lacking to
       a greater extent (26% : 31.5% respectively).

Over the period 1984-1986 the relative ranking order of Japanese and
Chinese appears ambiguous: neither features in the 1984 large-scale
survey of 'use', but both are 'in need' in the FLUNCI Surveys of 1984
and 1985. Japanese is ahead with 5% (1984) and 4% (1985), as against
2.5% and 2% for Chinese respectively. Infact, interest in exporting to
Japan appears to have suffered when the difficulties of penetrating the
Japanese home market became more apparent following the initial
experience of companies like Cable & Wireless plc. The convenient
location of Hong Kong-based agents, often serving the Far East region
as a whole, has also contributed to a somewhat greater focus on China.
The percentage of the sample using outside translation agencies for
Japanese and Chinese averaged 6.5% and 5.3% respectively over
1984-1985, which compares with 9.6% and 19.2% in 1985/6. Even

allowing for the use of a more controlled sample in 1985/6, there has been a sharp, and sudden increase in the need for, and use of, Chinese amongst Northern companies, which would probably put demand for it on a par with Japanese across a broader sample of industry.

The Minority Middle Eastern And Oriental Languages

Whilst the three most recent surveys of Northern industry point overall to a clear need for the four major Middle Eastern and Oriental languages, they also indicate a role for several other lesser known languages or language groupings. In order of importance these are Farsi (Persian), "Indian", Hebrew, Thai, Malay, Indonesian and Turkish. The term "African" was included by several respondents, but no evidence of a need for local African or tribal languages has been found in the North, except in the case of Rowntree Mackintosh plc, which prints a company report in Xhosa.

A number of companies trade with Iran despite political difficulties, which combine with the trade figures for the Middle Eastern region as a whole. More specifically, in the 1984 and 1985 surveys, two companies required translations for Farsi in the field of ferrous metals and one in mechanical engineering. In the most recent 1985/6 study, three companies had apparently used Farsi for business in the previous few years, one through a translation bureau. A fourth company in the same study also had a Farsi-speaking agent representing their business interests in Iran.

A more confusing picture emerges with reference to "Indian" languages amongst respondents: it is unclear to what extent this includes Urdu, Bengali and other languages of the Sub-continent. In the 1985/6 survey two companies out of 73 did not increase their trade performance for lack of "Indian" languages and three other companies claimed to have used a translation bureau for them. Not so encouraging is the relatively low proportion of British-born Indian language speakers using their language skills in Northern companies: only one company had used Urdu for business abroad. Apparently, the region's foreign trade has yet to benefit in any substantive way from the presence of the pool of immigrant and British-born speakers of these minority languages, or, at least, speakers whose mother tongue is closer to Indian or Oriental languages than English is. One simple explanation may be that many Northerners of Indian and Chinese origin tend to work in specific sectors; eg retail, or in small businesses, where foreign language use for export is not so great.

Very few companies appear to have any in-house expertise in Middle Eastern and Oriental languages; only Arabic and Chinese have shown up. A number of companies indicated that English-speaking agents were generally expected to handle any problems in the local language on the spot. Otherwise companies looked to their local university, or private language school, for specialist help in handling linguistic difficulties at home (see Fig 3):

FIG. 3:   **RELATIVE PREFERENCE FOR PROVIDERS OF LANGUAGE SERVICES FOR MIDDLE AND FAR EASTERN MARKETS (N = 73)**

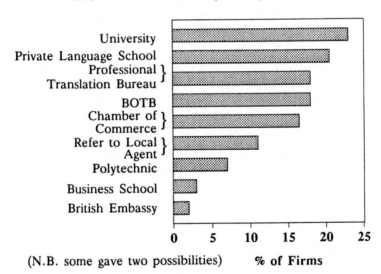

(N.B. some gave two possibilities)   **% of Firms**

Even with an awareness of these providers, several companies indicated the problems they experienced in getting trade and technical literature in brochure form translated and printed in these languages. One firm, for example, had been unable to make a promotional video for the Chinese market due to a lack of local expertise. Indeed, there were widespread difficulties evident throughout industry with acquiring high–quality sales literature in foreign languages.

Despite the relatively high percentage of companies looking to Higher Education, language departments are only now slowly coming in tune with industry's language needs. Even in graduate recruitment, there appeared to be no evidence of any noticeable entry of graduates of any discipline with skills in Middle Eastern or Oriental Languages into local industry. It remains to be seen whether new investment in university departments following the UGC Enquiry under Sir Peter Parker will bring any direct benefit to the manufacturing sector of industry and other exporters in the North of England. On the other hand, the North East Language–Export Consortium has the potential to satisfy industry's short–term needs, provided that inter–institutional rivalry does not impede progress.

Which Sectors Need Languages?

Whilst it would be glib to argue that all commerce and industry need languages, it is nonetheless true that companies are increasingly touched by the internationalisation of trade. Few businesses of any size can afford not to recognise Europe as their domestic market. But this message has yet to reach the broader workforce, particularly those in the region working in the public sector. For the average person, languages have only a minority value across the top ten sectors of regional employment given in Fig. 4, especially when viewed from the commanding heights of Education, Health, Public Administration, Defence, Energy and Water Supply, which have up to 354,000 employees on their local payroll. On the other hand, in the other areas of potential language use, such as the retail and hotel industries, there has been a marked reluctance to appreciate the value of foreign language skills. For example, only one retail chain has ever approached Newcastle Polytechnic to set up a short training course in Norwegian for shop assistants, while Collinson's Cleveland study (1981:101) made three disturbing discoveries about the poor international image of Cleveland's most prestigious hotels:

–   From 21 hotels contacted no–one provided a brochure in a foreign language.

–   Six hotels provided a menu in French with an English

translation. One hotel provided a menu for breakfast in French and German.

–   Only one hotel produced a key card in a foreign language.

**FIG. 4:   EMPLOYMENT OF INDUSTRY GROUP:
NORTHERN REGION**

Sector

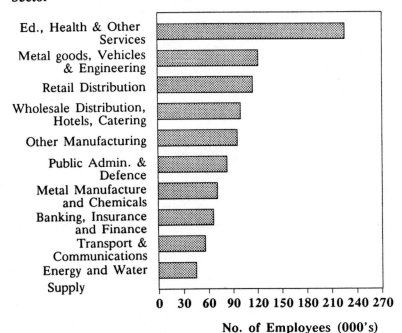

No. of Employees (000's)

Source: Department of Employment

Collinson's group also found that limited use was made of languages within the Local Government Service; there appeared to be no language specialisation and *ad hoc* arrangements were used where necessary (pp105–106). However, when an urgent and serious need does arise – such as the pre–investment inspection visit by representatives of Nissan – the regional and local industrial promotion agencies, NEDC (now NDC Ltd.) and Cleveland County Industrial Promotion Section, can show a serious commitment to foreign language use. In this case the Japanese were succesfully wooed in their own language; literature was translated, including business cards, a promotional film was dubbed into Japanese and the NEDC's Japanese agent was brought over to act as interpreter. At the time, however, all the translations were provided by firms based in the South of England, rather than in the North East, and foreign language type-settings were also commissioned outside the region (Collinson, p.109).

It is perhaps indicative of the seriousness with which the Nissan visit was viewed in the North East that such great efforts were made to use the Japanese language. Were this exceptional principle to be applied more extensively in the service sector – wherever foreign visitors are encountered – eg. tourist offices, railway stations, car hire, hotels and so on – more non-English-speaking tourists might well be attracted to the region. Sadly, all too few in the service sector are aware of the potential commercial benefits to be gained by conscious and deft use of foreign language brochures and notices, not to mention training receptionists to speak French, German, Norwegian and Swedish.

Other sectors, especially manufacturing, are particularly aware of language use. Table 4 below provides a comparison between 18 different industrial and commercial sectors in North East England and Cumbria. Sector 7, mechanical engineering and metal equipment manufacture, is particularly important, underlying the traditional engineering base of the region. In this sector the need for languages is particularly acute; that is not to say that German, French and Spanish linguists *per se* will necessarily be welcomed with open arms, rather there is a special need for engineers who can also operate in European languages other than English.

Similarly, specialists in chemicals/vinyls/plastics with German, Spanish (for Central and South America) and/or French could be well rewarded. Despite the comparatively low sample for each language, a pattern of the sectors emerges where French is useful: engineering, electronics and chemicals, followed by most other areas of manufacturing, particularly textiles, clothing and footwear. German is similarly widely used across these sectors, confirming the rough parallelism of application of these two major languages – few firms would want only one of these languages, most would prefer both.

TABLE 4: FOREIGN LANGUAGE USE AND NEED BY SECTOR

	Major Languages					
	German		French		Spanish	
	'Use'(%) N=143	'Need'(%) N=30	Use% N=132	Need% N=38	Use% N=36	Need% N=18
1. agric/forestry	–	–	–	2.5	–	5.5
2. mining/quarrying	3	–	2	–	2.8	–
3. food/drink/tobacco	6	–	6.5	–	2.8	–
4. chemicals/vinyls/ plastics	18	–	4.5	8.0	16.7	16.5
5. fine chemicals/ pharm	0.5	–	14.0	–	2.8	–
6. ferrous metals	4.5	–	2.0	–	5.6	–
7. mech.eng./ machinery	9.5	26.5	21.0	26.0	33.3	44.5
8. electrical eng.	8	–	7.0	5.0	11.1	–
9. marine/heavy eng.	5	–	6.5	8.0	8.3	5.5
10. instrument/ precision eng.	3	6.5	3.0	5.0	–	5.5
11. electronics	3	6.5	4.5	8.0	2.8	5.5
12. textiles/clothing/ footwear	13	10	8.0	5.0	5.6	–
13. domestic goods	9	13	6.5	5.0	–	11.0
14. misc. manuf.	6.5	6.5	20.5	5.0	11.1	–
15. R & D	1.5	–	2.0	–	–	–
16. services	3	6.5	5.0	–	–	5.5
17. printing	5	–	2.0	–	5.6	–
18. construction	2	–	–	–	2.8	–

N.B. Data on 'use' is taken from Survey 4 in Table 1 and data on 'need' is from Survey 6 in Table 2.

The key areas where German is used, apart from chemicals and mechanical engineering, are textile, clothing, footwear and domestic goods manufacture, electrical engineering and food, drink and tobacco. Central and South America is a particularly difficult market to penetrate without   Spanish, but there are major opportunities to export heavy industrial goods, bulk chemicals and plastics.

The main Arabic–speaking markets fall into the following categories: (1) chemicals/allied; (2) services/consultancy; (3) food, drink and tobacco; (4) electronics; mechanical engineering and construction/civil engineering. It is characteristic of Arabic that, though it is widely in demand, its use is variable: most companies argue that knowledge of the *language* may not be essential in trading with Arabic speakers, but understanding the culture carries major advantages. A number of companies would welcome an Arabic–speaking technologist on their workforce – one who understands the culture and commercial practice of the Middle East and is able to evaluate, hire and fire local agents when necessary.

Interestingly, one quarter of these companies needing Arabic also claimed to have someone on their staff who had developed some knowledge of the language; i.e. 6.5% of the total sample of 151 in the 1985 survey. Considering the region's extremely advantageous trade links with the Arabic–speaking world, especially with Saudi Arabia and the Gulf States, the virtual absence of Arabic language and culture as a school subject and the negligible provision at undergraduate level is a matter for great concern. Out of the 138 firms surveyed in the 1985 survey, 35.5% gave specific details of export contracts with either the Middle East or the Gulf. In the 1984 survey the percentage was virtually identical (35.7%). Despite the upsurge of interest in Far Eastern languages over recent years, the proportional demand for Arabic remains much higher than for Japanese and Chinese: in the 1985/6 survey the ratio was 5:2 (Ar:J) and 5:3 (Ar:Ch) in the Northern Region. The Arabic–speaking world is valuable market for Northern industry which is worth protecting and fostering, especially by equiping future British business people with a knowledge of Arabic and Arab customs and culture.

By comparison, the Far East is a relatively new and fast growing market. Demand for Japanese is apparent in the mechanical and heavy engineering sectors; food and drink; chemicals/allied; electrical and electronics; services/consultancy; textiles and automotive industries. Chinese is less broadly needed: mining and mechanical engineering;

chemicals; electrical and electronics; and precision engineering. In the 1985 Survey 15 Northern Companies (10.9%) indicated having signed export contracts with Japan and three with China (2.2%), a further ten companies (7.2%) exported to the "Far East". In the previous year, 1984, 9 companies (5.4%) declared they had exported to Japan, 7 to China (4.2%) and 22 (13.1%) to the "Far East"; i.e. a slight levelling off of trade with the Far East over 1984–5 at about 20% of both samples over two years. Clearly, if industry is to take advantage of the potentially vast Chinese market now opening up, far greater effort should be made to cultivate a greater regional capability in Chinese language and culture.

What are the Commonest uses of Languages in Business?

Businesses use foreign languages in a variety of ways depending on a vast range of variables; company sector, department within company (overseas sales, research and development etc.), nationality of customer, mode of contact (letter, telex, face to face etc.), company policy, place of contact (in U.K., on shop floor in foreign factory), availability of linguists on staff, type of transaction (buying or selling) and level of transaction (initial stage, informal stage, signing of contract) and many others.

In plotting the skills, sub–skills, functions, strategies and 'gambits' in foreign–language transactions, precise terminology had to be sacrificed in favour of more mundane, but accessible, descriptive categories, such as 'reading letters/telex', 'using the phone'. 'wining and dining' and so on, which were far more likely to provoke a response than, for example, questions framed in the metalanguage of linguistic transactional analysis. The generalised order of activities requiring foreign language use in Table 5 (below) is largely, predictable except, perhaps, for the predominance of 'reading' (i.e. comprehension of the written word) over other skills. It is certainly the case from talking to many personnel that the sheer volume of items written in a foreign language crossing many businesses' desks makes this skill more important than the others in terms of the *frequency of use* alone.

This should cause language syllabus writers food for thought since reading comprehension is often the forgotten fourth language skill. The range and extent of reading skills required varies from understanding detail in telex, correspondence, invoices, data sheets and shipping–documents to scanning a research article for valuable research data. These sub–skills seem not only lacking in business, but also hardly ever appear on undergraduate language degree courses. Although practice varies from company to company, employees with even the barest qualifications in foreign languages can be asked, by default, to handle complex documentation – with sometimes disastrous results.

TABLE 5: THE PRINCIPAL USES OF FOREIGN LANGUAGES

Order	Language Activity	N = 168 1984 %	N = 151 1985 %	Average ('84+'85) %
1st	Reading letters/telex	63.7	61.5	62.6
2nd	Travelling abroad	56.5	47.5	52
3rd	Using the phone	44.5	40.5	42.5
4th	Writing letters/notes	42	34	38
5th	'Wining & Dining' (social chat)	41	31	36
6th	Reading tech/sales lit	30	29	29.5
7th	Writing trade docs.	28	22	25
8th	Listening to talks	10	6	8
9th	Giving talks/speeches	9	6	7.5
Open	Customer meetings	3.5	3.5	3.5
Nil Response		7	14.5	

Fig. 5 (below) illustrates the different set of activities where the four leading non–European languages were most used for business purposes in the 1985/6 sample, though rarely by the company's own home–based employees. For Arabic, Japanese, Chinese and Korean, most companies rely on outside assistance (hired translator, interpreter, local representative or local agent) to perform language operations. This accounts for the distinction between 'translation' and 'reading' in Fig. 5; 'translation (written)' means the word–for–word translation of technical documents, foreign trade literature, data sheets, research articles and patents into English; i.e. those which cannot be read, or even scanned, by the companies' own personnel. In the same sample of 73 only six claimed they had some in-house skills in Arabic, three in Chinese, one in Japanese and one in Persian; none had skills available in more than one exotic language. Companies frequently have to resort to guesswork in deciding whether an item arriving in a rare foreign language should be sent outside for a costly translation, left at the bottom of the in-tray and treated with deliberate circumspection, or simply shredded.

The availablity of personnel with foreign language skills in Northern firms varies considerably depending on the language. By and large, companies rely on whatever linguistic skills their staff already have (usually a reflection of school provision), but the more internationally-aware ones train against need as, and when, they enter a new market. In the 1985 'FLUNCI' Survey, 96 companies out of 151 claimed some languages expertise, but 55 had none. In other words, one third of Northern companies engaged in foreign trade may have nobody capable of using a language other than English for business abroad. Of the 96 with some language skills, 31 had skills in only one language, another 31 had two languages and 34 had three or more languages. In most cases the two-language firms had French and German, but the level of competence was little more than a 'rusty O-level'.

It is perhaps not fortuitous that in addition to the 151 responses received from the 1985 Survey, 42 nil responses came back marked 'not applicable' and 24 envelopes were returned unopened to the sender with the note, 'gone out of business'! There is a strong possibility that a proportion of these defunct businesses failed due to their inability to respond to, or even recognise, orders sent in a foreign language, or understand customer enquiries phoned through in a language other than English.

FIG. 5:   ACTIVITIES/SKILLS WHERE ARABIC, JAPANESE, CHINESE AND KOREAN ARE USED

Key

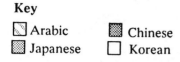

□ Arabic   ■ Chinese

■ Japanese   □ Korean

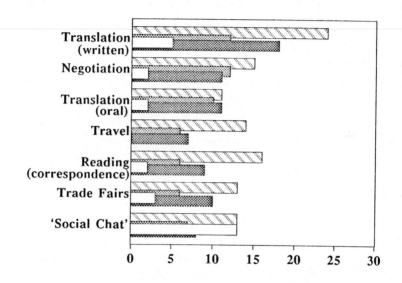

No. of Firms (1985/6 Survey)

TABLE 6:   COMPANIES CLAIMING PERSONNEL WITH
FOREIGN LANGUAGE SKILLS

In-House Languages	N = 168 1984 %	N = 151 1985 %	N = 118 1985/6* %
No language competence	24.4	36.0	90.7
French	61.9	50.3	N/A
German	49.4	44.4	N/A
Spanish	22	18.5	N/A
Italian	17.9	11.3	N/A
Dutch	7.1	5.3	N/A
Arabic	6.5	2.0	5.1
Swedish	4.2	4.0	N/A
Norwegian	3.0	1.3	N/A
Danish	2.4	2.6	N/A
Japanese	2.4	2.0	0.8
Chinese	1.8	0.7	2.5
Russian	1.8	0.7	N/A
Portuguese	0.6	1.3	N/A
Others: Urdu, Finnish, Hebrew, Indonesian			

* this survey concerns only deep-sea trading companies and the
use of Arabic, Japanese and Chinese.

The *level* of in-house language competence across different business
situations has not been verified within this study, but it ranges from a
'smattering' to native-speaker quality. Indeed, the existence of
speakers of Scandinavian languages and Dutch is principally due to
branch plants of Dutch and Scandinavian companies employing their
own nationals locally. The returns for German, Spanish, Italian and
Arabic, which are higher than would be expected from school
provision, suggest that acquisition of languages needed at work, but
often missing from schools, has been taking place in other ways. The
overall picture is, however, very depressing for a manufacturing region
seeking to expand its export markets abroad. The failure of the LEAs
in the region to provide either the necessary languages or the most
useful language skills in our schools over the last twenty years was often
cited by respondents as the major reason for the nation's recognised

ineptitude in speaking languages other than English. The most frequent vituperative remarks levelled at schools, usually by business people over 30, concern what they allege is the failure of schools to teach them how to *speak* the language in everyday situations. They decry the failure to treat a foreign language as a *living* medium and the seeming irrelevance of the language to employment, or to courses in subjects other than languages at university or polytechnic.

However, it should be said that much of the criticism should have been levelled at the Examination Boards, which, for generations, preferred grammatical accuracy to practical communication. In Higher Education throughout the country, too, admissions procedures have seemingly underpinned the apparent *irrelevance* of languages by relaxing specific foreign language requirements for admission to courses in the sciences and social sciences. The myth of irrelevance has been given further credibility by the tendency in some Science and Technology departments to axe the foreign language option on the grounds that 'liberal arts' *(sic)* are dispensable during periods of retrenchment. Foreign language education in Britain has traditionally suffered at the hands of parochially–minded administrators and academics who see language skills as a mere 'general studies option' – on a level with domestic science, or 'learning to play tennis', as one respondent put it.

Given the region's industrial profile, the case of Russian in this context is both tragic and illuminating; pruned to extinction in many universities (e.g. Newcastle) over the past ten years, the Russian language and associated Soviet and East European Studies have now reached a point of critical shortage.* Government and UGC arguments for the rationalisation of Russian into a few centres still fail to grasp the widespread need for languages, such as Russian, across the curriculum in Science and Technology. It is this kind of short–term uninformed thinking which has so often epitomised high–level educational decisions – to the detriment of industry and commerce in the long term. As for Russian in Northern trade and industry, years of retrenchment may account for why no more than *three* companies out of 168 in the 1984 sample and *one* out of 151 in 1985 had someone with skills in Russian – fewer than for Swedish or Danish, and putting it only one place above Portuguese in Table 8.

---

* See "Trade chiefs in crisis talks on Russian shortage', *THES*, Headline, 4/12/87.

Outside Agencies and Agents: How Important?

The paucity of personnel with adequate language skills in local companies and the frequent mismatch of available skills to business needs lead to reliance on outside translation bureaux and local agents abroad for language–related tasks. In the 1985 sample of 151 companies, 62% indicated they had used a translation bureau within the previous three or so years. In 1984 the figure was even higher at 71%. Such findings on translation agencies in Figures 6 and 7 reveal virtually the same pattern of foreign language demand which is evident from responses to Q4. The order of demand is also the same for each survey apart from the place of Russian, which displaces Chinese for seventh position in 1985. Other languages where translation services were required are (in order of frequency): Dutch, Swedish, Norwegian, Korean, Portuguese, Hungarian, Greek, Farsi, Finnish, Polish, Roumanian, Thai (Siamese) and Serbo–Croat. Amongst Middle and Far Eastern trading companies surveyed in 1985/6, the order was Arabic (19%), Chinese (11.9%), Japanese (5.9%), Korean (1.7%), Farsi (1.7%) and Thai (Siamese) (0.8%), confirming the primary importance of Arabic within the 'exotic' group. However, only 30% in this sample had used an outside bureau, leaving the local agent to handle many of the day–to–day business transactions with customers in their local language.

The role of local agents requires particular attention: firms which have no knowledge of the local language or culture find themselves over–reliant on their agent abroad. Transactions are carried out through the agent , who acts as both interpreter and adviser; sales reps sent from the U.K. can find they have very little direct contact with the end user. More disturbingly, when the agents are on commission and handling business from several companies, they may have no more loyalty to the British supplier than to the German or Italian manufacturer who produces the same, or similar, products. The British supplier can lose out on two fronts: the choice of agent has to be one with good English first and technical or market knowledge second. Secondly, evaluation of the local agent should be handled by a British sales rep who speaks the local language. Since this is a rarity in most non–English speaking markets, the performance of the local agent can only be assessed on *actual* sales figures, which may fall short of *potential* sales, without the British company realising it.   Market research abroad is also often left in the hands of the local agent and the U.K. company gives up any means of direct intelligence gathering. The widespread use of agents is disturbing and requires further evaluation.

USE OF TRANSLATION AGENCIES

Fig 6: 1984 (N = 168)   **Fig 7: 1985 (N = 151)**

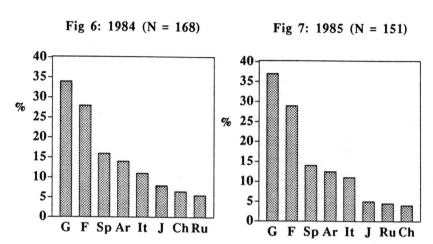

Even in 71 transactions with French–speaking countries in the 1985 Survey, 35 were through a local agent;* i.e. half. When the market is further afield, or more linguistically and culturally inaccessible, the percentage goes up. In Arabic–speaking countries the percentage rises to 70.6% in the same survey. Further afield still, the percentage is more difficult to quantify, since many companies have a Far East agent based in Hong Kong, whose territory takes in China, Japan and South East Asia.

The percentage of British companies employing a local agent for each *language* of the Far East out of all companies trading with each language area, or country, in the 1985/6 survey is given in Table 7 (below). Collinson *et al* (1982:82) found that between 42% and 44% of companies in their sample of North East businesses, outside Cleveland and in Cleveland respectively, carried out sales through a local agent. They similarly noted the same upward trend for the Middle East (p.89).

---

* or occasionally through a hired interpreter.

TABLE 7: PERCENTAGE OF COMPANIES EMPLOYING LOCAL AGENT FOR FAR EASTERN MARKETS

Language	% Companies with Local Agents	
Chinese	59.1%	(N = 22)
Japanese	60%	(N = 15)
Korean	55.6%	(N = 9)

(where N = total of companies trading with each language area)

Taking the last four studies of the North East into account, an approximate estimate would be that about as many as 50% of the firms exporting to Europe rely on local agents, rising by a further 10%–15% to up to 65% for the Far East and the Middle East. Employing local agents abroad is very common business practice. However, if – as it appears – local agents also have a monopoly over the dialogue with customers and end users, too, then monolingual English–speaking companies have to take far too much on trust than is commercially wise, especially during transactions.

The Language of Commercial Transaction

It is a commonly held fallacy that English is used throughout the world as the *lingua franca* of international business. Whilst this is true in many cases, findings from the Northern surveys paint a more mixed multi–lingual picture.

First, there is no denying the importance of English: Germans often use English in the Far East when dealing with the Japanese; Koreans negotiate ship–building contracts in English with Venezuelans. It would also be foolhardy for any British company to attempt to negotiate the terms of a legally–binding agreement in a language other than English, to do otherwise could risk errors costing the company substantial sums of money. On the other hand, it is always well–received to use the customer's language at suitable moments during transactions and especially on social occasions. Tables 8 – 11 detail the languages of transaction with French, German and Spanish–speaking countries.

TABLE 8: LANGUAGE OF TRANSACTION BETWEEN NORTHERN FRENCH-SPEAKING COMPANIES AND EXPORTERS

Survey Year	No. of Export Transactions Cited	% in English	% in French	% Mixed Fr. & Eng.
1984	85	47%	40%	13%
1985	71	32.4%	55%	12.7%

TABLE 9: LANGUAGE OF TRANSACTION BETWEEN GERMAN-SPEAKING COMPANIES AND NORTHERN EXPORTERS

Survey Year	No. of Export Transactions Cited	% in English	% in German	% Mixed Eng. & Ger.
1984	71	42%	45%	12.7%
1985	85	62.5%	28%	9.4%

TABLE 10: LANGUAGE OF TRANSACTION BETWEEN SPANISH-SPEAKING COMPANIES AND NORTHERN EXPORTERS

Survey Year	No. of Export Transactions Cited	% in English	% in Spanish	% Mixed Eng. & Sp.
1984	45	55.6%	35.6%	8.9%
1985	24	66.7%	16.7%	16.7%

TABLE 11: LANGUAGE OF TRANSACTIONS BETWEEN ARABIC-SPEAKING COMPANIES AND NORTHERN EXPORTERS

Survey Year	No. of Export Transactions Cited	% in English	% in Arabic	% Mixed Eng. & Ar.
1984	56	75%	17.9%	5.4%
1985	43	79%	9%	11.6%

On average, Northern companies carry out approximately half of their export transactions with the Near Continent in English andthe proportion of English rises further in the non–English speaking world beyond. The figures for transactions with Spanish–speaking countries show a rise of between 5% and 10% in the use of English, whilst, for Arabic–speaking countries, at least three–quarters of the transactions are conducted wholly in English. Moreover, transactions conducted in the local language show a greater participation by local agents; in French–speaking countries, for example, where we would expect a higher degree of linguistic self–sufficiency on the part of British companies, local agents or local interpreters were used for between 56% and 75% of the transactions held in French.

Three points arise from this: firstly, one cannot, nor should not, assume that **all** transactions can be carried out in English – even in the non–English speaking countries nearest to our shores. Secondly, despite the well known maxim that the customer's language should be used when exporting (except, of course, during the negotiation of finely–detailed contracts and agreements), it is surprising how relatively little this applies in reality. Thirdly, a number of transactions, and contacts, are carried on in a **mixture** of languages; English **and** the local language. This can vary between about 9% and 16% of the transactions, which suggests that, for many British business people, listening comprehension skills are of particular importance; ie they speak in English but the other side reply in the local languages*. It is also worth remembering that even if the language of transaction is deliberately chosen to be English, local buyers will still tend to discuss the offer in a whisper, or in an aside, with colleagues in their own language – providing invaluable clues to any secret strategy the other side might be adopting. This can be a major bonus for the British negotiator who understands the local language, but does not reveal it.

As a general rule, good export practice may be summed up as not only **knowing** the customer's language, but **knowing when and how** to use it, or **not** use it, to greatest effect. Apart from this, the myth should finally be laid to rest that English is enough and can always be the language of transaction between British exporters and foreign companies; the data here on **successful** contracts show a substantial proportion are in the customer's language, or a mixture of languages, especially in France and Germany.

---

*Evidence of this 'mono–dialogue' is also corroborated by Collinson (1982:26)

What is the Relationship between Language Needs, Exporting and
the Company Profile?

It is possible to identify certain categories of company which are more
likely to have foreign language needs; the most relevant variable are
variables annual turnover, percentage of goods exported to
non–English speaking countries and sector. The sector with the largest
need tends to be engineering (especially mechanical) within
manufacturing, as has already been discussed. An average of just
below one–third of companies in the samples which declare they need
languages fall within the range of £1–5 million in annual turnover; ie
companies no longer bracketed as 'small businesses' in the North East,
yet which are smaller than 'medium–sized'. If we take the range £¹/₂
million – £10 million, this takes in 49% and 61% of the two samples
respectively. The smaller business sector with an annual turnover of
under half a million should also not be dismissed; 22% and 17% of the
samples come into this classification. What appears to be the case is
that the need diminishes in large companies with a turnover of over
£20 million pa. In the 1985 survey only two respondents with declared
language needs had a turnover in excess of £100 million pa.

TABLE 12: EXPORT PROFILE OF LANGUAGE–NEEDING
COMPANIES

% Output Sold Abroad*	% Companies Needing Languages	
	1984 (N = 91)	1985 (N = 66)
0% – 10%	51.5%	50%
11% – 20%	12%	10.5%
21% – 30%	18.5%	13.5%
31% – 40%	4.5%	6%
41% – 50	5.5%	1.5%
51% – 60%	1%	4.5%
61% – 70%	3.5%	4.5%
70%+	4.5%	7.5%

(NB percentages have been rounded up to the nearest half)
* to non–English speaking markets

The percentages given in Table 12 clearly show a consistent picture across the two surveys: the majority of companies which are 'language–needing' export under a third of their goods to non–English speaking markets. What is interesting here is that the companies in the samples have all given lack of foreign languages, yet these are as a reason for not significantly improving their level of trade, are the companies most aware of the value of foreign languages. There are certainly greater numbers of companies unaware of the role of foreign languages who wrongly blame the competitiveness of their product or delivery dates for their lack of foreign sales.

Languages and Importing

There is perhaps a general tendency to assume that *selling* should be done in the customer's language, which means *buying* goods into Britain needs no foreign language expertise. However, only a minority of the 1984 survey sample (42%) were purely exporters. The majority were engaged in both exporting and importing with non–English speaking markets. The rationale for more effective importing is self–evident. Buying goods abroad is clearly essential to maintaining the bouyancy of the country's export performance. For example, machinery, raw materials and semi–finished products are often unobtainable in this country and have to be bought from abroad involving lengthy market research, searches, visits and meetings. The value of the foreign language then lies mainly in maintaining the necessary rapport with the supplier to ensure not only the lowest possible price, but also the best possible service and delivery terms.

The foreign supplier can be as important to a company as the export outlet; if British buyers cannot speak the local language, they are *less likely* to change their suppliers than if they do speak the language. For example, when a new price list is sent over, or when there are supplier problems, British companies are often unable to despatch a rep to the area who speaks the language well enough to seek out an alternative supplier quickly. Moreover, when the goods are sent by road transport, there can be untold difficulties of communication with foreign distribution depots. Almost all transport managers have horror stories to tell of foreign   drivers telephoning through to their homes in the early hours of the morning with a message delivered in garbled English and a panic–stricken   voice concerning some unintelligible catastrophe that has beset them, or their cargo, somewhere en route.   At these moments happy is the manager who has enough words of a foreign language to solve the matter quickly and quietly without resorting to ever-increasing decibels of loud, repetitive English shouted down the receiver!

Where does the Future lie?

It is certain that markets will change, and so will the corresponding need for different languages. However, it is unlikely that the region's present need for German and French will decrease in the forseeable future. As already indicated, the pattern of demand for the region's first five foreign languages has been consistently the same over a number of years: German, French, Spanish, Arabic and Italian.

In Table 13 the relative importance of the same language-areas can be seen in the individual export contracts indicated by companies in the 1984 and 1985 surveys. Firms listed the countries/regions where they had exported goods in the previous year and the size (in £ million) of the sale in each country. In Table 13, the 1984 respondents mentioned 453 separate export contracts in 22 non-English speaking countries or regions of the world. In 1985 the figure was 378. The region's links with Scandinavian countries and the Dutch-speaking Low Countries show up here more strongly than elsewhere in the study. One possible explanation is the well-known tendency in those countries to speak English. This introduces a factor which should not be overlooked: if trade is relatively easily carried out in English provoking customer resistance, such as in Scandinavia, then committing time to learning just a few words of greeting or pleasantry in the local language could be all that is required to produce proportionally far greater returns.

The same principle of a high return per unit of time invested also applies to Arabic, Chinese and Japanese. Yet herein lies the major dilemma not only facing the Northern Region, but also the country. Few schools provide any grounding in these languages and cultures at all. On the other hand, the prospects for trade between the North of England and the Middle East and Far East do not appear to be diminishing. In Fig.8, respondents declared where they foresaw greatest trade growth. Although nearly 80% mentioned Western Europe, the Middle East/Gulf was the second most quoted zone. The single most quoted country was Germany, thus confirming the continuing predominance of German in the region.

TABLE 13: NUMBER OF INDIVIDUAL EXPORT OUTLETS FOR GIVEN LANGUAGE AREAS

Country/Region of Language Area	1984	1985
German–speaking	66	67
French–speaking	65	65
Middle East	60	49
Spanish–speaking	40	23
Italy	24	16
Sweden	23	17
Far East (unspecified)	22	10
Dutch/Flemish	21	29
EEC/W Europe	19	12
Scandinavia (unspecified)	17	16
Norway	14	13
SE Asia (unspecified)	13	5
Denmark	10	8
Africa (unspecified)	11	9
Japan	9	15
E Europe	8	4
Portuguese–speaking	8	4
Greece	7	4
Chinese–speaking	7	6
Korea	5	2
USSR	2	4
Indonesia ,	2	0
Total	453	378

FIG. 8: PROSPECTS FOR TRADE GROWTH

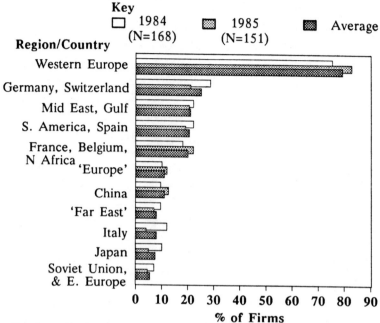

Key
□ 1984 (N=168) ▨ 1985 (N=151) ▨ Average

Region/Country

Western Europe
Germany, Switzerland
Mid East, Gulf
S. America, Spain
France, Belgium, N Africa
'Europe'
China
'Far East'
Italy
Japan
Soviet Union, & E. Europe

0 10 20 30 40 50 60 70 80 90
% of Firms

(Under 5%: S E Asia, Sweden, Norway, Portugal, Greece, Indonesia

What can be done?

The issue facing the Northern Region is how to deal with the obvious mismatch between employers' foreign language needs and educational/training provision. Is it realistic to propose the introduction of languages like Arabic, Japanese or Chinese into schools and colleges? These are particularly hard languages where progress is slow and fluency a difficult goal to attain, except for the few who are linguistically gifted. Since there are wide variations and dialects within Arabic and Chinese, depending on the country or location, it would be inappropriate even with purely utilitarian motives to set up large–scale learning programmes in Classical Arabic, or Mandarin Chinese, as the two varieties closest to standards in the two 'language regions'. Indeed, Classical Arabic is little closer to many current varieties of Arabic in North Africa, the Middle East and Gulf than Latin is to French, Spanish or Italian.

Currently, however, without any grounding early on, training to speak fluent Arabic, Chinese or Japanese in later life is, for many business people, a virtual unreality. Short, intensive language courses are often a last–ditch attempt at gaining enough understanding to survive travelling and social or lightweight meetings abroad, whilst retaining a modicum of self–respect. They treat the symptoms, not the disease, and their value quickly diminishes without further, and regular, consolidation over a longer period or, better still, an extended stay in the country. Grafting on language skills in later life, or training against need, is not the best long–term solution. Fundamental changes have to occur in the schools and colleges of the region; young people should at least acquire the capacity at school to learn languages more effectively in later life for when the actual need arises. Programmes to induce linguistic awareness should be more systematically developed, on the basis of which pupils would be more receptive to language sound and structure systems other than French. Briefings and courses in Middle Eastern, Oriental Studies or Latin American Studies could be made more available, where the culture and language–type of the particular world region are examined. It would also be defeatist not to earmark particular schools for special provision in Arabic, Chinese and Japanese. Other countries have managed to achieve this, such as Sweden and the Soviet Union, and the capacity of many British school children to learn hard languages has been underestimated too frequently in the past. It is more a question of stimulating motivation and providing the resources.

The North–East Language Export Consortium, based at Newcastle Polytechnic and funded jointly by DES 'PICKUP' and the MSC, is a welcome attempt by Central Government at tackling the region's foreign language dilemma. Its existence should provide companies with a more finely–tuned, better resourced and locally–oriented foreign language and export service, able to draw upon regionally–based expertise in such languages as Arabic, Chinese and Japanese, as well as the major European ones. However, the LX Consortium has yet to convince industry that it offers a higher quality, wide–ranging and more competitively priced service than the private sector. Perhaps more important, it has to convince companies of the combined commitment of its member institutions (universities, polys and colleges) to supporting local firms by adopting a demand–driven approach which reflects the changing needs of industry in the 80's.

At present the greatest mismatch concerns foreign language choice. Little hope exists for initiatives on 'Language and Culture' modules, if LEAs, advisers and the HMI seem powerless even to introduce European languages other than French into the school curriculum. French is almost as important to the region as German, but it alone cannot satisfy the country's undisputed need to speak, listen or export to the world beyond Paris, Brussels, Casablanca or Libreville. It remains to be seen, however, whether the school sector can provide more than the present minority of communicatively–competent speakers in languages other than French without the imposition of a centrally–organised quota system on schools and colleges in the region. Otherwise, future generations of British travellers outside France will be condemned to shouting more loudly at uncomprehending foreigners in English, just as they have done in the past.

SUMMARY

1   An increasing number of companies in the Northern Region of England are using foreign languages for trade and a sizeable proportion has recognised that their inability to operate in certain languages has *significantly* affected their performance;

2   The order of importance of languages in the region is consistently (1) German (2) French (3) Spanish (4) Arabic and Italian. The main application is for reading correspondence, travelling and telephoning, but the principal need is for personnel with business or professional qualifications who have *additional* language skills to offer;

3   Certain types of company in the region are more likely to have foreign language deficiencies; namely, those in engineering or metal goods manufacture, companies which export less than 30% of their output and smaller companies with a turnover of less than £10 million pa;

4   Despite a high proportion of companies claiming to have in–house skills in two or three major world languages, there is substantial reliance on outside agencies and, in particular, on local agents for language–related business at home and abroad. Translation bureaux can be prohibitively costly, especially for Oriental languages.

5   Local agents can exercise greater control over a company's affairs than is commercially healthy due to their monopoly of access to information in the local language. There is a proportionally greater dependence on agents in territories outside Europe, especially the Middle East. Companies often have one Hong Kong–based agent serving the whole of the Far East;

6   Importing in a foreign language can sometimes be as important as exporting – especially where foreign suppliers and purchasing agreements are concerned, or where communication difficulties with foreign distribution depots or drivers may aries;

7   The region's present patterns of export outlets are not expected to change in the late 80s; most companies look to expansion of business with Germany and France; Western Europe is the region of first choice, followed by the Middle East. Growing opportunities also exist with the Far East and Latin America;

8   There is a clear mismatch between educational provision and industrial need. Since the school sector seems powerless to offer a range of core languages to the majority despite evidence of demand from employers, there is little hope of matching provision to need amongst the present generation of school leavers;

9   In short term, the new Language–Export consortium promises a more coherent and relevant response to industry's language needs from within Further and Higher Education, but it has yet to prove that is can deliver the right service at the right price.

NOTES

1   *Survey Nos. 1 & 4* involved all company–types without pre–selection of exporters or for language users. *Survey 3* was aimed at probable users, principally in Cleveland, though 31 of the 76 positive respondents were in the North East outside Cleveland.

The data for 1 and 4 are extracted from the "Directory of Employers in the Northern Region", an internal publication of Newcastle Polytechnic's Appointments and Careers Advisory Service, produced in 1977 and revised in 1984.

Survey 2 was carried out by Paul Perkins at Newcastle Polytechnic's Department of Modern Languages and *Survey 3* is recorded in "Foreign Languages in Businesses in Cleveland 1981", an unpublished DMS dissertation submitted to Teesside Polytechnic in 1982 by M Collinson, P.A. Hanage, P.W. Readman and J.M. Wilkinson, whose support is gratefully acknowledged.

2   *Survey 5* is based on a questionnaire (see Appendix 1) sent out to approximately 2000 local companies, employers and organisations with the assistance of the North of England Development Council and the Tyne and Wear Chamber of Commerce, whose encouragement is gratefully acknowledged. The resulting sample of 168 users is 'random' insofar as the Author had no control over the selection or classification of individual companies contacted. The response rate was 12.05%, due to the high proportion of local employers initially contacted who were not involved in export and import, such as retailers, and the exclusion of trade with the USA and the Commonwealth.

Survey 6 is based on the response to the same questionnaire sent to c.850 exporters of all types in the region. The response rate was 17.8% and like *survey 5*, the questionnaire was largely irrelevant to trade with the USA r the Commonwealth. *Survey 7* focussed purely on 'deep sea' trade with Africa, the Middle East and Far East (Appendix 2). The response rate was significantly higher at 37.1%; 118 replies from the 320 exporters contacted.

3   The data submitted to the UGC enquiry was based on only 44 companies which had replied by the deadline. A further 29 companies later produced information during December 1985 – January 1986, increasing the total sample to 73 users of African and Oriental languages for the present study.

Chapter 2

FOREIGN LANGUAGE DEMANDS OF FIRMS IN THE YORKSHIRE AREA
Kate Chambers

Regional Profile

The Yorkshire area[1] and parts of North Humberside provide a survey picture of contrast and rapid change across the full range of local industry. Traditional and established textile and engineering industries have had to update and diversify in response to present-day demands, while many new companies have sprung up in electronics, plastics, petrochemicals, healthcare and biotechnology.

One dominant feature of the region is its strong European outlook on the East Coast with four international ports, (Hull, Immingham, Grimsby and Goole) leading over 250 international companies from more than 13 countries to establish manufacturing and service bases within the region.

Whilst the centre-spring of the region's commerce and industry is clearly Leeds and Bradford, where the majority of people live, there is a thriving small and medium-sized business sector dotted around the rural areas of the Dales and North Yorkshire Moors.

Survey Respondents : Trade Profile

The survey of foreign language users was carried out at Leeds Polytechnic in early 1987 using Steve Hagen's questionnaire.[2] Out of 410 companies mailed, a total of 86 companies responded positively on the use of languages – a response rate of 21%.

As Table 1 indicates, a majority of the positive respondents trade in the two key traditional manufacturing sectors of the region – mechanical engineering and the textiles, clothing and footwear sector. However, the rising importance of electronics to the region's trade shows up clearly in the order of exports, whilst, at the other end, only one language user is evident from the service sector.

TABLE 1

Industrial Class	Percentage of Firms Exporting (N=86)	Percentage of Firms Importing (N=86)
Textiles/clothing footwear	23.3	15.1
Mechanical engineering	16.3	14.0
Instrument/precision eng	10.5	7.0
Electronics	7.0	5.8
Miscellaneous manufacture	7.0	5.8
Electrical engineering	7.0	4.7
Chemicals/allied	5.8	8.1
Agricultural/forestry	2.3	2.3
Ferrous metals	2.3	1.2
Mining	2.3	–
Food/drink/tobacco	2.3	–
Marine/heavy engineering	2.3	–
Domestic goods	1.2	1.2
Services	1.2	–
Fine chemicals/ Pharmaceuticals	–	1.2
R & D	–	–
Other	14.0	15.1

eng = engineering

Our sample further indicates that many companies in the region tend to look to the home market first for their sales, before seeking export abroad.

Table 2 shows that 59% of our sample obtain over 50% of their sales in the UK whilst only 14.1% export over half their goods to non–English speaking countries and even fewer firms (3.6%) to English–speaking countries. The discrepancy between these latter two figures is itself significant, emphasizing the underlying trend in British trade away from the old traditional markets towards non–English speaking countries, especially in Europe.

Foreign Language Demands Of Firms
In The Yorkshire Area

By contrast in Table 3, a majority of companies in the survey (59%) import from English–speaking countries, as opposed to non–English speaking countries (24.6%). When examining changing trading patterns, the real and potential value of foreign language skills in penetrating new markets is increasingly apparent.

Table 2

THE PERCENTAGE OF RESPONDENTS SELLING TO DIFFERENT MARKETS AS A PROPORTION OF THEIR TOTAL SALES (N = 86)

Goods sold to	% of firms with variable sales			
	for: 1%–25% (of sales)	26%–50% (of sales)	51%–70% (of sales)	71%–100% (of sales)
(a) The home market	13%	28%	19%	40%
(b) Other English–speaking countries	61.2%	12.8%	2.4%	1.2%
(c) Non–English speaking countries	56.5%	17.6%	17.6%	5.9%

(NB 22.4% of our sample did not trade with English–speaking countries and 11.8% indicated zero for trade with non–English speaking countries)

Table 3

THE PERCENTAGE OF FIRMS BUYING FROM DIFFERENT AREAS AS A PROPORTION OF THEIR TOTAL PURCHASES (N = 86)

Area of purchase	% of firms with variable purchases			
	for: 1%–25% (of purchases)	26%–50% (of purchases)	51%–70% (of purchases)	71%–100% (of purchases)
(a) The home market	9.4%	3.6%	14.1%	60%
(b) Other English–speaking countries	33%	4.6%	2.3%	1.1%
(c) Non–English speaking countries	60%	3.6%	3.6%	6.2%

(NB 59% of respondents did not buy from other English–speaking countries, while 24.6% appeared to purchase nothing from non–English speaking countries)

The Language Needs Of Survey Respondents

A majority of companies (60%) responded positively to Question 4, indicating under–performance for lack of "foreign language facilities".

However, the firms in need are concentrated in Leeds and West Yorkshire, whilst the Bradford and North Yorkshire samples are evenly divided.

Table 4 SURVEY RESPONDENTS IN NEED OF LANGUAGE BY AREA

Sample area	% 'yes' (i.e. in need)	% 'no' (i.e. not in need)
Leeds	26.5	11.5
N. Yorks & Humberside	12.5	12.5
Bradford	11.0	11.0
W. Yorks	10.0	10.0
Total	60%	40%

The pattern of foreign language demand reflects the overall rank order of French (19), German (17) and Spanish (15), which, perhaps not so surprisingly, illustrates the clear need for German – almost equal in demand to French.

Table 5   FOREIGN LANGUAGES IN DEMAND

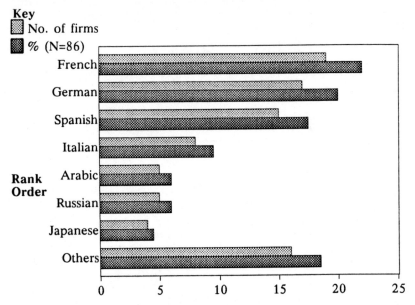

The rank order of the first two placings is reversed when examining companies' use of outside translation bureaux. Out of the 51 firms who had employed outside assistance, 53% needed German, and 43% – French. Interestingly, after Spanish (37%), Arabic and Japanese come equal fourth (14%), followed by Russian (12%).

Language Of Transaction

The main language of transaction was overwhelmingly English for import and export. Of those who answered this question 67 examples of English were given as the language used in export. The next most frequently used languages were, in order of importance; French (26 cases); German (24 cases); Spanish (14 cases) and Italian (13 cases). Other languages used in export transactions included Hebrew, Portuguese, Chinese, Arabic, Japanese, Dutch and Scandinavian languages.

Asked about the language used for import transactions, one respondent whose firm appeared to use only English in all transactions, stated, "I have yet to come across any firm which doesn't use English for import transactions". Presumably, many of our counterparts abroad would express the same sentiment about buying in their own language from abroad, too! Our results showed that while English was used in 53 cases, some companies were still making efforts to use the foreign languages for imports. Not surprisingly French and German were used in eight and seven cases; but an unusual finding was the use of Italian by 7 firms. Among the respondents 47 indicated that they had used a local agent (or interpreter) abroad; in these cases English was not used for transactions. The main foreign languages used were German and French, but eleven other European and non-European languages were also listed.

In analysing the answers to this section of the study it would have been interesting to establish a connection between the use of language and trade success in relation to the approximate value of goods to and from different countries. However, a number of respondents declined to answer all or part of this section. Some stated that such information was confidential and one firm stated firmly, "It would take a long time to work out all this and we are very busy", thus highlighting one of the principal reasons why large, empirically–based studies on language use in industry have been so few in number.

Outside Dependency and In-house Resource

The majority of our sample, over 59%, had bought in the services of an outside translation/interpreting service during the previous three years. Of the 51 individual cases, only 1 was abroad, 50 were in Britain, including 14 who used services from both 'here and abroad'. Table 6 indicates a pattern of need similar to other parts of the country, with German most in demand at 31.5% of the sample:

Table 6   USE OF OUTSIDE AGENCIES FOR GIVEN
           LANGUAGE

Key
☒ % Question–respondents (N=51)
▦ % Total sample (N=86)

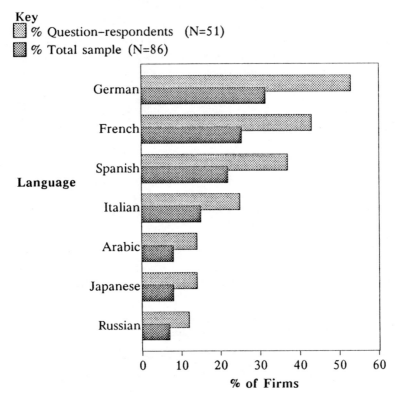

Other languages used included Dutch, Polish, Chinese and Hungarian.
However, the use of professional services is not necessarily an indicator
of the respondents' inability to function in a given language. In a
number of cases professionals were used for languages known to
members of the firm. This could be interpreted as evidence for firms
setting very high standards of foreign language performance for certain
business purposes, where clear precision and accuracy were
paramount.

Companies' own ability to use languages was by no means lacking
either. The vast majority of respondents to this question had used their
own staff for French (90%) and German (71%),whilst skills in Spanish
and Italian (each 28%) were clearly present, despite the paucity of
provision at school. There was evidence of companies using Arabic
(6%) and Russian (4%), though the level and extent of utilisable skills

in these languages were not examined. In 6% of cases harder languages had been used, such as Finnish and Hungarian —though principally by local agents acting on the firm's behalf.

Use Of Languages

The manner in which foreign languages are used (Table 7) similarly falls into the pattern of British companies in other surveys, although 'wining and dining' is here given particular prominence. This confirms the impression gathered informally that the social use of foreign languages is of special importance and underrated on many courses. British business people may often be entertained in the company of people whose English is inadequate, and they often regard it as a courtesy at least to attempt social conversation in the foreign language.

This appears to be true particularly in cases where high–level business transactions are conducted in English. Whilst the remarkable proficiency in English of many overseas business people makes it likely that English is the language of transaction, at other, more relaxed times, it can be a positive advantage to socialise in the local language to cement the busines relationship. Despite this, in certain countries it is not uncommon for business people with foreign language ability to find themselves obliged to speak English to please their customers. "It's often necessary to let them practise their English on us" was a comment made by several respondents on the survey. However, in spite of the widespread use of English, it is often the case that last–minute arrangements, emergencies or changes of plan can only be handled in the foreign language. This survival use of foreign languages for travelling, phoning and so on, is mentioned as 'very important' by several respondents who travel regularly in Italy, Germany France and Latin America.

Perhaps a surprising feature of these findings on language use is the relatively high proportion of respondents who list 'writing letters in a foreign language' as important. It may be that professional translators are employed by some firms for this purpose, while other firms may realise the importance of responding in the foreign language, though, in practice, may not have the skill to do so in every case. Moreover, since the turn–over of even short pieces of work sent to a translation bureau can be at least as long as a week, companies – sometimes erroneously – consider a prompt written response in English to be a better market strategy than a slower response in the foreign language.

Table 7   THE PRINCIPAL ACTIVITIES WHERE COMPANIES USED A FOREIGN LANGUAGE IN TRADE CONTACTS WITH FOREIGN FIRMS

Activity/skill/situation	Important	Very Important
1 Wining and Dining (Social Chat)	78%	6.4%
2 Reading letters and telex	59%	17%
3 Writing letters/notes	52%	7.7%
4 Travelling abroad	50%	23%
5 Using the phone	49%	14%
6 Writing trade documents	43.5%	5%
7 Reading tech/sales lit	19%	6%
8 Listening to talks	14%	0
9 Giving talks/speeches	10.3%	1.2%
10 Others (Business meetings, negotiations)	10.3%	1.2%

Patterns Of British Trade

The changing pattern of British trade is clearly apparent in the respondents' level of interest in Western Europe. In total, 28 out of 78 question–respondents (36%) looked for future growth to Europe, or one country/region of it. Perhaps rather ominously, 21 companies declined to pinpoint any of the world's regions for future growth. As for the optimists, Table 8 indicates the leading growth areas of the future as Western Europe, South America and the Far East.

**Table 8   RESPONDENTS' PROJECTED TRADE GROWTH
AREAS**

REGION/COUNTRY RESPONSES	No. OF POSITIVE
Western Europe/'Europe'	**36**
West Germany	14
France	12
Spain	11
Italy	7
Benelux	4
Scandinavia	4
Turkey	2
South America	**16**
Far East	**11**
China	8
Japan	5
Middle East	**9**
Eastern Europe	**5**
USSR	1
Africa	**4**

SPECIFIC CASE STUDIES: THE POLYGLOT TEXTILE FIRMS OF WEST YORKSHIRE

Attached to the competed questionnaire from a Bradford firm, H Dawson Sons & Co (Wool) Ltd, were the comments of Geoffrey Padgett, Head of Export Sales, "Such a survey is long overdue, as is action to rectify the lazy UK attitude to languages". A close look at the questionnaire indicated that this firm had an unusually high level of language awareness with regard to trading activities. Their own staff included speakers of French, German, Spanish and Italian. They had used interpreters both at home and abroad for Russian, Arabic and Japanese. They also claimed to have lost trade through lack of German, Japanese and Arabic. For Geoffrey Padgett there was no doubt that to sell abroad successfully meant going out and learning the languages, "Whenever possible we try to use the language of our buyers. All the time we use languages, especially German, French and Italian. In textiles, historically, we have the attitude that you get out and sell in the customer's language". Although language, according to him, should be used at all levels, it is of inestimable value in just establishing a rapport with customers, "If you're in touch with them on the 'phone or telex and you tell them in their languages, 'I saw your football team on TV last night', you're showing them you're interested, and it all helps".

Geoffrey Padgett's words were confirmed by the findings of the survey for twenty textile firms in the Bradford area. From their response a definite and distinctive pattern emerged, showing a higher level of language awareness than any other category of firms in the study; sixteen of the twenty firms used a foreign language in the transaction of business. All but two firms had foreign language speakers on their staff (these two firms used interpreters). Of the three firms having only one foreign language speaker, two were French–speaking, the other Italian. It was found that nine firms had at least three languages: three spoke four languages and one firm was able to work in five foreign languages. Of all languages used, French was the most widely known (17 firms); German (14 firms); Italian (12 firms); Spanish (5 firms) and Arabic (2 firms).

The concern for foreign language use was further confirmed by their use of interpreters. Eleven companies had used interpreters, mostly at home, for the four main European languages and for Japanese. An interesting observation was that in several cases professional interpreters had been brought in even for languages which were spoken by the company's own staff. This suggests that either they could not match up to the linguistic skills required in a particular field, or that the company were setting themselves a very high standard in the use of language for certain transactions. One company which regularly used an interpreter, as well as having knowledge of foreign languages, claimed nevertheless to have lost business through lack of 'all languages'. Another firm able to offer five foreign languages, used interpreters but still claimed to have missed out on business deals, even though it managed to export 95% of its production! These views appear to represent the opinion among the companies in general of the vital importance of foreign languages in import and export.

In West Yorkshire and, in particular, in Bradford, textile companies have had to diversify and imports of raw materials now include more trade with China, Japan and other countries in the Far and Middle East. The main export market is, however, still Western Europe. Traditionally, training for many young salesmen at the outset of their career has included work experience in some of the textile towns of Germany, France or Italy. For many companies reciprocal arrangements have enabled trainee salesmen to work with agents or customers in centres such as Prato or Biella.

Concluding Remarks: Languages And The Individual

With increased international movement in multinational companies, relocation of middle and senior management to associate companies abroad has become widespread. For many, learning a new language has become an essential part of the challenge of a new position. Not only will language skills be needed in work, but ease of day-to-day living could be considerably enhanced for the individual and his/her family with access to the necessary competence in the foreign language.

One recent student at Leeds Polytechnic Modern Languages Centre, William McDonnell, a management accountant at ICI, was transferred to Rouen for 2–3 years with only 13 days available to build up his French from a 'rusty' 'O' level. His needs were very specific: "In my French course the emphasis had to be on getting my information across. All my technical product information had to be put over in French." On the last day of the course, he seemed confident about his ability to cope: "At first it was difficult for me to appraise the level I'd have at the end, but it's given me confidence to speak, so it's been very worthwhile."

The language barrier frequently assumes greater proportions in the mind of the learner than they are in reality. Chris McDermott of

Johnson Radley, who took a six–week intensive course in French prior to departure, found the anticipation was worse than the event. "The great thing was, and I didn't realise until I got there, there was enough for me not to freeze." He had no doubt that his ability to deal in French had proved decisive. He believed one could only sell to the French if it was a product they did not have;

"In this case it's helped enormously being able to speak French to them. My French is adequate for what I need and I think that my customers wouldn't like to be in my position, just dropped in to Leeds and having to speak English. So you gain their respect and it helps to fill the gaps, even if you're not word–perfect."

Mr Grainger of West Yorkshire Engineers acquired German adequate to reach the right person when going on a 'cold start' visit to Germany and recently got the business of a firm whose previous Italian supplier spoke no German. For Mr Grainger using a language is an essential courtesy:

> "If someone came to my office and spoke only German, I'd show him the door. If you're going to do business in someone else's country, you should have the decency to try to speak and understand their language."

With these words Mr Grainger sums up what is an essential, but simple, message for British industry – one which has not yet reached all the companies it should.

References and Notes

1. Here, principally N. and W. Yorks, including Leeds and Bradford.
2. See Appendix 1.

Chapter 3

LANGUAGES IN THE INDUSTRY AND COMMERCE OF HUMBERSIDE
Dr Gertrud Aub-Buscher

Profile Of The Region [1]

The county of Humberside, carved out during the reorganisation of the English counties from East Yorkshire and the north of Lincolnshire, is made up of two distinct sections, divided by the River Humber, though now linked by the Humber Bridge : North Humberside, with Hull as its focal point, and South Humberside, which includes several large conurbations, notably Grimsby/Cleethorpes and Scunthorpe. It is an essentially agricultural region : 1,152 square miles, i.e. 85% of its total area of 1,356 square miles, is agricultural land, and 49% of that is classed as grade 1 or 2. The total area allocated for industry is 33,081 hectares. And yet a mere 4% of its total employed population of 337000 in 1984 was engaged in agriculture and mining[2], while 90% worked in services (59.3%) or manufacturing (30.7%) industries.

The industries in the county cover a wide range; 90% of the Standard Industrial Classification's Minimum List Headings were represented in 1981. The major manufacturing industries are food and drink, chemicals and allied industries, steel, and aeronautical engineering. Among the major concerns in the area are the British Steel Corporation, British Aerospace, Birds Eye, and Reckitt & Colman. However, 94% of companies are small businesses employing fewer than 50 persons.

The greatest concentration of service industries is in commercial and professional services, followed some way behind by the distributive trades, utilities and transport. Transport is perhaps the activity which marks the region more than any other. The Humber Estuary handles 10% of all trade through British seaports. In 1984 Immingham ranked 6th among British seaports in terms of the value of goods handled, and Hull was 10th. To these must be added the cargo which goes through the ports of Grimsby and Goole, and the over 11 million tonnes handled by private wharfs, bringing the total tonnage passing through in 1984 to 43.9 million, and the total value to £11,491.5 million. The ports were used by 446,417 passengers in 1985. 125,500 more passed through Humberside Airport, located on the Southbank at Kirmington and growing steadily since the opening of the Humber Bridge in 1981.

62 countries are served regularly from the Humber ports, from Peru to Taiwan, from Iceland to Tahiti. 33,209,000 tonnes or just over 75% of the total goods

handled in 1984 represented foreign trade, 23,693,000 (71%) being imports and 9,516,000 (29%) exports. Liquid bulk with over 9 million and dry bulk with just over 8.5 million tonnes accounted for the major share of the imports, dry bulk (3.5 million) and liquid bulk (3 million), containers and roll-on goods (2 million) led the exports.

The Survey

A preliminary survey of language needs in industry and commerce in the Humberside region was carried out in the spring of 1986 in collaboration with Dr E. A. McCobb of the University's Department of German. Of the 126 members of the Institute of Freight Forwarders and the Institute of Export who replied to our questionnaire, 9 considered knowledge of a foreign language 'essential', 23 'important', 85 'useful', and only 6 'irrelevant'. Neither the response rate nor the attitude to languages was as positive in the current survey.

The Sample

A total of 805 questionnaires went out in late November and early December 1986, as follows:
–   85 to those members of the Institute of Freight Forwarders and Institute of Export who had responded to our previous survey giving their names and addresses. 74 of these were in Humberside, 11 from neighbouring counties.
–   23 to representatives of major firms in the area who did not figure among the 85 mentioned above.
–   97 to members of the Grimsby Chamber of Commerce who were known or likely to be involved in exporting activities.
–   600 (approximately) inserted in the regular mailing of the Hull Chamber of Commerce.

94 replies were received, 15 as blanks, indicating no involvement in trade or one so minimal that most of the questions were meaningless. 6 forms were filled in by firms either not engaged in foreign trade or whose export targets were all in the English-speaking world. ('English-speaking' in the normal sense of the expression, not the sense attributed to it by one respondent who considers the whole of the EEC as anglophone territory...)   65 of the replies came from

Humberside, 58 from north of the river and 7 from the South Bank. The others were from North Yorkshire (2), West Yorkshire, South Yorkshire and Cleveland (1 each), and 3 failed to give an address. Only 73 responses hence came from firms which could clearly be said to have practical experience of trade with countries where English is not the normal vehicle of communication. This figure underlies the report of results which follows. It includes 10 firms whose experience lies in the area of imports only, and 11 for whom exports to non–English–speaking areas account for less than 10% of sales. Three firms are represented twice, in one case by different branches, in the other two by different members of their staff; as the answers given were by no means identical, they have all be included.

Not all respondents answered all questions or all sections of them. Gaps were particularly frequent in sections concerned with volume of exports and imports and with turnover. One firm stated explicitly that it was not company policy to divulge this sort of information. 50 forms (68.5%) contained an indication of company turnover. Though the figures given are subject to caution, in that only some answers made it clear whether the sum given refers to the Humberside branch or to a larger parent company, a rough analysis is given in Table 1.

TABLE 1: Profile of Responding Companies by Turnover

Turnover £	No. of Companies	% of sample
0 – 1 million (incl.)	14	19.2
1 – 10	18	24.6
10 – 20	3	4.1
20 – 30	5	6.8
30 – 40	2	2.7
40 – 50		2.7
over 50	5	6.8
'in the large company range'	1	1.4
Not indicated	23	31.5

Foreign Trade Activities

Nearly all respondents gave some details of their trading activities. The exceptions were two who indicated that their activities were too widespread to be specified, and one for whom questions were not applicable, as 'English is spoken in all the countries where I trade.' However, numerous gaps in the answers mean that full correlation between all the variables is not possible.

1. **Trading partners**, though they ranged all over the world, were mainly concentrated in Europe. Given the sometimes very general answers, they are listed in Table 2 quoted as they were mentioned:

TABLE 2: Chief Trading Areas of Firms in Sample

Region/Country	Number of firms	
	Exporting to	Importing from
West Germany	22	19
Holland	17	16
France	13	9
Belgium	11	11
Scandinavia	9	3
Europe	8	6
Switzerland	7	5
Italy	6	7
Spain	6	3
EEC	4	3
Japan	4	1
Benelux	4	–
Arab Gulf	4	–
Denmark	3	6
Finland	3	5
Austria	3	4
USSR	3	2
Far East	3	1
Middle East	3	–
North Africa	3	–
Norway	2	5
Sweden	2	4
Portugal	2	2
Greece, Latin America, Yugoslavia	2 (each)	1 (each)
Mediterranean	2	–
Brazil	–	4

2. Not surprisingly, shipping and haulage dominated the list of **goods and services** traded, as shown below:

TABLE 3: Industrial Sector of Good Traded

Industrial Class

KEY
▓ Exporters
▓ Importers

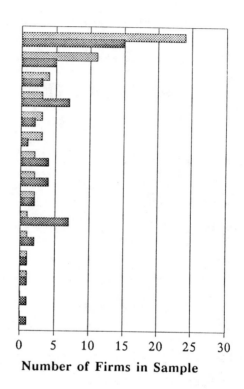

services: shipping/haulage
Other (misc.)
chemicals/allied
mechanical engineering
misc. manufacture
other
food/drink/tobacco
electrical engineering
electronics
agric/forestry
ferrous metals
fine chemicals/pharm.
marine/heavy engineering
textiles/clothing/footwear
R & D

0   5   10   15   20   25   30

Number of Firms in Sample

3. Only 42 respondents (57.5%) indicated *the value* of their exports or imports or both, and it is therefore open to question whether the distribution shown is below typical of the sample as a whole :

4. 50 forms (68.5%) contained information about the countries considered to be **potential areas of growth** for the firms concerned, with one further respondent indicating that it all depended on circumstances and another including the whole world. The following countries/areas were mentioned:

TABLE 4: Value of Goods Traded

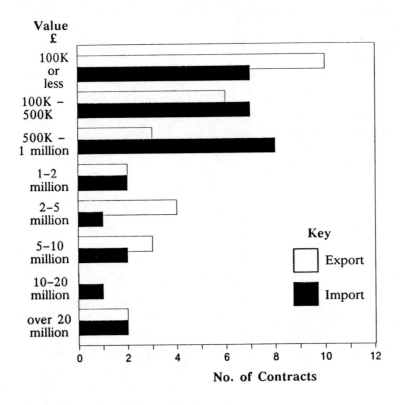

TABLE 5: Potential Trade Growth

**Main Regions of Potential
Trade Growth**   **No. of Firms**

	(a) Giving Region	(b) Already Trading in Region
Spain	12	5
West Germany	11	9
Western Europe/EEC/'Europe'	7	7
Scandinavia	5	5
France	5	3
Far East	5	2
Middle East	5	1
China	5	1
Holland	4	2

Italy	4	2
South America	3	1
Portugal	3	1
Sweden, Finland, Iceland	2 (each)	2 (each)
Denmark, Africa	2 (each)	1 (each)
Greece	2	–

With 63 mentions (48 of them for EEC countries), Western Europe is hence seen as the area of future expansion by twice as many firms as the whole rest of the non–English–speaking world combined.

Perceived Language Needs And Use

It would appear from the survey that English is still very much the language of foreign trade. For 29 trading contacts where the local language is used in export, there were 103 where all activities take place in English and 19 in a mixture of English and the foreign language. Among importers the relative figures were 21, 89 and 11 respectively.

The number of firms using particular foreign languages for specific transactions is in Table 6:

TABLE 6: Language of Transaction

Language of Transaction Total			No. of Specific Transactions		
	Exports		Imports		
	alone	with English	alone	with English	
German	7	7	5	7	26
French	5	3	3	2	13
Dutch	3	2	4	2	11
Spanish	3	–	2	–	5
Italian	1	1	3	–	5
Arabic	1	4	–	–	5
Greek	1	1	1	–	3
'Scandinavian'	2	–	–	–	2
Portuguese	1	–	–	–	1
Russian	1	–	–	–	1
'Yugoslav'	1	–	–	–	1
Japanese	–	–	1	–	1
Norwegian	–	–	1	–	1
Finnish	–	–	1	–	1
European (not specified)	4	1	–	–	

A very large proportion (52 respondents or 71.2%) indicated that firms had made **use of their own staff** or that of their head office in foreign trade over the past three or so years. The languages used were:

TABLE 7: In–House Language Skills

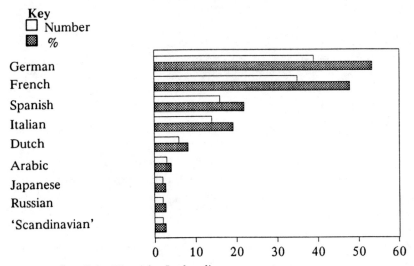

Key
☐ Number
▨ %

German
French
Spanish
Italian
Dutch
Arabic
Japanese
Russian
'Scandinavian'

0   10   20   30   40   50   60

Others: Swedish, Finnish, Icelandic, Chinese, Portuguese, 'Yugoslav'.

About half of the sample had at some time during the last three years made use of the services of a **translating/interpreting bureau** either here or abroad. Suggesting widespread reliance on outside assistance for language needs. Where the response was 72, 47.2% had used such facilities abroad and 47.2% had **never** used and agency.

Have used service here   :   34 (47.2%)
Have used service abroad :   7 (9.7%)
Have not used service   :   34 (47.2%)
(3 firms used services both here and abroad.)

The languages for which such services were used were :

TABLE 8: Demand for Translation Bureau

Language in demand	No. of firms	% of users of services	% total sample
German	16	42.1	21.9
French	12	31.5	16.4
Spanish	10	26.3	13.7
Italian	5	13.2	6.8
Arabic	4	10.5	5.5
Russian	3	7.9	4.1

Others: Chinese, Creole, Dutch, Greek, Icelandic, Korean, Nepalese, Pidgin, Swedish.

A total of 29 companies (39.7%) indicated that they use a **local agent and/or interpreter** in their trading especially for export.   22 firms returned a positive response (30.1%) on using an agent for importing, or for a mixture.   This use of agents (Table 9) was widespread throughout the world.

On the key issue of poor trading performance for lack of foreign languages 27 companies (37.0%) felt that they *could have significantly improved* their trade performance over the last few years if they had had access to foreign language facilities; 43 (59.0%) indicated that they could not have, the rest returning a nil response. Those who did regret the lack of access to language facilities gave the following languages as those that would have been useful:

**TABLE 9: Main Areas of Demand for Local Agent/Local
Interpreter**

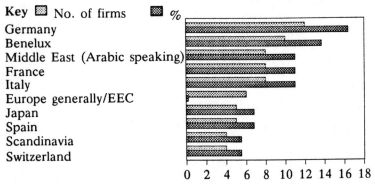

Key ▨ No. of firms   ▨ %

Germany
Benelux
Middle East (Arabic speaking)
France
Italy
Europe generally/EEC
Japan
Spain
Scandinavia
Switzerland

0 2 4 6 8 10 12 14 16 18

Others (2–2.5%): Far East, French, West Africa, Latin America
Portugal, Russian, Greece, Finland, Brazil.

Under 2%: Bolivia, Sweden, Norway, Denmark, Austria,
East Germany, Yugoslavia, Iran, New Guinea, Africa, North Africa.

TABLE 10: Firms Underperforming for lack of Languages

sample	No. of firms	% (N = 27)	% of total
German	16	59.2	21.9
French	14	51.8	19.2
Spanish	10	37.0	13.7
Italian	7	25.9	9.6
Arabic	6	22.2	8.2
Russian	4	14.8	5.5
Dutch	3	11.1	4.1
Japanese	3	11.1	4.1
Portugese	2	7.4	2.7
Danish	1	3.7	1.4
Icelandic	1	3.7	1.4
'Scandinavian'	1	3.7	1.4

In the following list of *principal activities* where foreign languages have
been used for trade and business, the figures in brackets refer to those
deemed 'most important':

TABLE 11: Principal Activities for Language Use

	No. of Firms	% of Sample
Reading letters/telex	46(8)	63.0
Travelling abroad	39(6)	53.4
Using the phone	32(3)	43.8
Writing letters/notes	28(2)	38.4
Wining & Dining	27(3)	37.0
Writing trade documents	15(2)	20.5
Listening to talks/speeches	11(1)	15.1
Reading technical/sales literature	11(–)	15.1
Giving talks/speeches	7(–)	9.6

Others (conversation with
drivers, exhibition work,
sales, sending telexes,
technical installation)

The question having been answered by 61 (83.6%) respondents,
potential language trainers should no doubt take note of the priorities
indicated.

Company Language Policy

Only 24 replies (32.9%) indicated that knowledge of a foreign language
is **an area of expertise sought for in the recruitment of staff**; for 45
(61.6%) it is not, though one firm indicated that a member of staff
proficient in French would soon be needed, and another would
consider a knowledge of French or Arabic a useful additional attribute
in the technical or sales departments. (4 forms were blank on this
question.) Insofar as it is possible to relate the positive answers to size
of operations as expressed in turnover, the distribution was as follows:

Turnover £	No. of firms	positive	%
0 – 1 mill.	13	5	38.5
1 – 10 mill.	18	5	27.8
over 10 mill.	18	10	55.6

The departments where expertise in languages is considered desirable are:

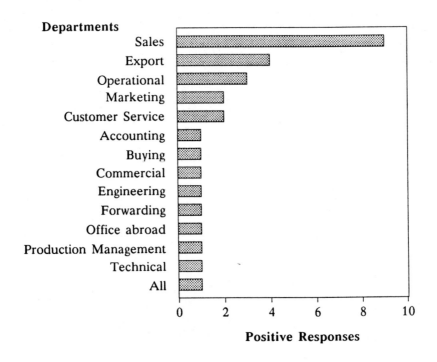

Departments

Positive Responses

Language training forms part of company policy for only 5 firms in the sample, a mere 6.8%. All of them combine training with recruitment policy. One of them is a small firm (turnover of less than £1 million), one has a turnover of between £1 million and £10 million, and the three others come from the large firms. Given the relatively small number of answers showing the volume of trading activity, a valid correlation between export performance and a language policy, at the level both of recruitment and training, is scarcely possible. For 9 companies with a positive language policy, figures on foreign trade are not available. These include three of the five firms which provide language training for their staff; for one of the two remaining, both exports and imports lie between £1 – 2 million, the other exports goods worth between £5 – 10 million.

Of the companies recruiting staff with a knowledge of foreign languages for whom figures are available.

the value of exports is:			for		the value of imports is:			for
£100k	or less		3		100k	or less		–
100k	–	500k	2		100k	–	500k	3
500k	–	1 million	2		500k	–	1 million	4
1	–	2 million	1		1	–	2 million	1
2	–	5	2		2	–	5	–
5	–	10	3		5	–	10	–
					10	–	20	–
					over 20			1

CONCLUSIONS

The almost exclusive concentration on the teaching of French as the first and often only foreign language in many schools should perhaps be reviewed, in this area at least. With 30% of all respondents exporting to West Germany and 26% importing from there, that country is clearly the most important trading partner for the region. To that must be added the other countries where German is the normal vehicle of communication : Austria, Switzerland (there was no evidence of trading partnerships with francophone Switzerland) and East Germany, giving a total of at least 33 (42%) exporting and 29 (39.7%) importing contacts with German speaking countries. These were second only to the Hispanic world as possible areas for expansion, and German consistently led in questions about language use or desirability.

This preponderant need for German is also borne out by requests for language training (courses and private study) received from local firms in our Language Teaching Centre. Holland follows closely, with 23.3% of the sample exporting and 21.9% importing. If to this we add the figures for Belgium (15.1% for each activity) and Benelux (5.0% for exports, no imports) we arrive at a total of 32 (43.8%) Dutch–speaking trading partners for export and 27 (37%) for importing. The answers giving information on language use in contacts with Belgium all mentioned Flemish, none French.)

France, with 17.8% of firms exporting and 12.3% importing, comes only in third place as a trading partner, and francophone countries outside of Europe do not increase the percentages significantly. French does, however, figure second in lists on languages actually used or seen as useful.

Greater attention to the teaching of Spanish is perhaps warranted by the number of times it was mentioned in replies. Actual trading with Spain itself is currently not high (8.2% and 4.1%) and nor are the figures for Latin America, but Spain was top of the list for possible growth, a position further enhanced by references to Latin America. Spanish was third or fourth for actual use, and third of the languages seen as potentially useful.

The second significant feature evident in the survey is the very important role played by Europe in the area's trading activities. To persons living in the region, the Continent, especially the Low Countries, often seems rather nearer than London. But the very low level of trading activity with the rest of the non–English–speaking world seems surprising in what many would see as an essentially seafaring region.

Lastly, it is perhaps the silences which speak loudest: the forms not filled in because all these questions are irrelevant, because shipping agents do not need languages, because the whole world speaks English. Will all the publicity given to the importance of language expertise by bodies such as the British Overseas Trade Board and the Institute of Export, to the insights gained by studying a trading partner's language to the magic effects of the good–will shown by even a stumbling greeting in the language of the possible buyer change all that?

References and Notes

1   Cf. John Siddall, *Humberside, Facts and Figures 1986*, available from County Hall, Beverley, North Humberside HU17 9BA, which has provided most of the information for this section.

2   Total population : 851,600.

Chapter 4

THE LANGUAGE NEEDS OF FIRMS IN THE WEST OF SCOTLAND
Margaret Ross

Scottish industry and commerce had traditionally been more involved in overseas trade than that of the United Kingdom as a whole; the history of Glasgow, the major city in the West of Scotland and indeed in Scotland as a whole, whose proud boast once was that it was the "Second City" of the British Empire, is the proof of that. We have not always had to sell in the language of our customers, but it has become imperative that we now do so. This does not mean simply stating our prices in francs, marks and lire, but means we need to be able to deploy market intelligence that is sensitive to the culture in which we have to compete.

Unfortunately, it is not as obvious as this to many of the firms in this area; our survey questionnaire (Appendix A)* revealed the weaknesses in the general approach of many local businesses to the whole area of foreign language use. Three factors have emerged which have affected export performance: firstly, a belief in the superiority of the English language (e.g. "all our foreign colleagues speak good English"). Secondly, there is heavy dependence on translation agencies – an expensive item, particularly for the small firm. Then there is often complete dependence on local agents, which can be a notoriously unreliable way of gathering market information and advice.

Background and Rationale

From the information provided by the Scottish Council for Development and Industry[1], manufacturing industry provides the main Scottish exports. In terms of the Standard Industrial Classification (SIC) Scotland's manufactured exports in 1984 came principally from the engineering industries (SIC 31 – 37) with the main exports within that category being office machinery and data–processing equipment worth between (£1000 million and £1100 million in 1984).

---

* At the end of this chapter.

The next largest sector is food, drink and tobacco industries (worth some 931 million in 1984), perhaps not surprisingly, in a country whose main export is automatically assumed to be whisky!

Though these figures appear fairly healthy – Scottish exports grew nearly twice as fast as UK exports in 1984 – they show only the good side of the picture. Even from the statistics supplied by the SCDI, it is clearly the large firms who have contributed to Scotland's recent comparatively successful drive in exports. The smaller firms not only have far fewer resources at their disposal, but also many demonstrate such a complacent attitude, particularly in the low value put upon in-house foreign language expertise as far as international trade is concerned, that it is likely that many of these small firms would not flourish in the field of exports. The worst example we came across of this was one firm who responded to the question on how their language needs were met, by writing in bold letters: "We shout loudly in English".

The most recent figures from the SCDI indicate that the main non-English-speaking importers of Scottish goods are, in order of importance:

TABLE 1

Country	£ Millions
West Germany	747
France	347
Netherlands	326
Japan	227
Italy	198
Sweden	147
Belgium	144
USSR	114
Spain	79
China	69

However, if we compare this order of priority with the situation of modern languages in Scottish Secondary schools, we see that no attempt has been made either to encourage the study of languages as a vital tool for industry and commerce, or even to parallel the needs of commerce by concentrating on the most important languages in terms of Scotland's major export markets. Were any of the above factors to be taken into consideration by educational planners, we would no longer have the automatic domination of French, followed a long way behind by German, then Spanish and Italian. Japanese would also figure in school curricula and Russian would have an important place, as well.

Our own experience, coupled with reports on Britain's poor overseas performance due to its lack of appropriately trained personnel[2], underlined our conviction that, in general, industry and commerce were badly served by the local universities and polytechnics. Their language graduates would often have great difficulty coping with straightforward language tasks within a firm: writing in an appropriate register and level of language to overseas companies, using telex, telephones and handling trade documents. In recognising industry's needs, Glasgow College of Technology responded by developing two distinct types of courses: one for languages graduates – suitably to retrain them and fully arm them to enter the world of industry and commerce. The other was in the form of in–house courses tailored to suit the local business community. Efforts in these two areas were directly concerned with helping Britain's overall export performance by making good the deficit within Britain's formal educational provision.

Sample and Survey Objectives

The Glasgow Chamber of Commerce provided a copy of their Master List of Exporters for the West of Scotland, i.e. 377 firms, to circulate with our questionnaire.

The survey objectives were to establish:

(i)   what foreign countries are the main trading partners for firms in the West of Scotland;

(ii) how many firms transact their business in English;

(iii) what degree of involvement the firm has in the use of foreign languages;

(iv)   for what activities within the firm are foreign languages
         perceived as necessary;

(v)   how these firms meet these needs at present.

In addition we asked firms to indicate what areas of linguistic expertise
they felt were most important to their firm. For this section we offered
a choice from commercial, technical, legal, marketing or other. We
also asked the firms to indicate their size: 1 – 50 employees, 51 – 500,
and over 500 employees. It was emphasised in the accompanying letter
that these questionnaires were anonymous, and that our interest lay
purely in the statistics.

From the 377 questionnaires which we sent out, 177 were returned to
us (47%), 17 were invalid for different reasons: e.g. the firms did not
export, or the information we requested was confidential. The
remaining 160 valid responses were analysed using the SPSSX package
to process the data.

Survey Findings
(i)   **The major trading areas:**
TABLE 2

Language/Trading Area	% of Respondents
French	83
German	81
Italian	60
Spanish	55
Arabic	52
Japanese	41
Portuguese	37
Russian	19

It is apparent from these high percentage figures that the companies in
the West of Scotland sample trade extensively with non–English
speaking countries. When these results are compared to those of other
surveys, it is also clear that one major difference between our figures
and others is the relatively higher place of Italian in our 'league table'.
This is, however, easily explained by demographic reasons, namely the
relatively high proportion of people of Italian origin who chose to settle
in the West of Scotland, as compared with other regions in the United
Kingdom.

(ii) **Firms who transacted their business in English:**

TABLE 3

Language/Trading Area	% only English
Japanese	95
Arabic	94
Russian	90
Portuguese	90
German	82
Italian	81
French	74
Spanish	68

Clearly the overwhelming majority of firms used English, not the foreign language, as the language in which to transact their business.

(iii) Our findings on the **degree of firms' involvement in the use of the foreign language** were equally clearcut. We had offered the firms four possibilities to express their involvement:– 'substantial', 'frequent', 'infrequent' and 'occasional'.

By taking the 'substantial' and 'frequent' figures together, and expressing them as a percentage of the total involvement figures (i.e. taking all four categories together) we have the following results in order of importance:

TABLE 4

Substantial/Frequent use of	% of firms
French	44
German	38
Spanish	35
Italian	12
Arabic	6
Portuguese	4
Japanese	3
Russian	2

These figures again reflect the pre-eminence of French in the Scottish secondary school sector. German and Spanish trail behind and the other foreign languages are nowhere in sight. They also indicate a very bleak picture when we look in particular at the trading areas which, according to the SCDI statistics, are amongst our main trading partners here in Scotland. Japan, a country to whom we at present export £227 million worth of goods per year, is particularly badly neglected in linguistic terms in the West of Scotland. Virtually no attempt is made to conduct business in Japanese, and Japanese is not taught in local schools.

We next looked at the figures indicating in what areas the firms involved in our survey felt that the use of the foreign language was necessary. We had again offered a choice of four activities that an exporting firm might be expected to be concerned with; 'personal contact with foreign colleagues'; 'interpreting'; 'translation into the foreign language'; 'translation from the foreign language'.

Of the firms who expressed an opinion about which was the **most important** category of use: 55 firms rated 'personal contact'; 46 rated 'translation from the foreign language'; thirdly, 14 firms rated 'translation into the foreign language'; finally, 3 firms rated 'interpreting'.

However, the findings on the individual firm's own involvement in these activities shows a different set of priorities:

– translation from the foreign language	80% of respondents found this their main involvement in use of language
– personal contact	76% of respondents found this their main involvement in use of language
– translation into the foreign language	65% of respondents found this their main involvement in use of language

| – | interpreting | 50% of respondents found this their main involvement in use of language |

This order of activities parallels that in other surveys; the London Chamber of Commerce and Industry Survey came up with translation from the foreign language (reading reports/correspondence) as being their priority, closely followed by personal contact (conversation with one person), then translation into the foreign language.

In terms of the most important areas of linguistic expertise, the figures showed that there was also a clear order of importance: the largest proportion of the firms – 45% – said that the commercial domain was the most important for them; 23% chose marketing as the area in which expertise in the foreign language was most required; 13% needed the foreign language in the technical domain and 1% of firms need foreign language expertise in legal matters.

(iv) **How language needs are met at present** : this issue is of particular interest, since our initial feeling was that firms who are obliged to rely on the services of a Language Agency or Translation Bureau would find this to be an expensive item over the course of a financial year.

Over the spread of eight languages mentioned in our survey, the results showed that translation bureaux were employed as follows:

–	translation into the foreign language	all languages
–	translation from the foreign language	all except Russian
–	interpreting	Arabic, French, German Spanish and Russian
–	personal contact	French

This clearly indicated a substantial dependence on the services of agencies and therefore an appreciable element of cost, particularly for the smaller firms who were on the majority of those responding to the survey. Of the 160 valid replies to our survey, 49% of the firms had 1 – 50 employees; 78% firms had 51 – 500 employees and only 12% came into the over 500 employees category.

Conclusions

Firstly, the findings were pessimistic: it is clear that firms in the West of Scotland are in the habit of using English as their main trading language. Unfortunately, some are clearly quite content to do so, to judge by the unsolicited comments on some of the questionnaires, e.g. under "needs met" companies had written, briefly and to the point, "no need for foreign languages" or had indicated that their contacts spoke English. The chief message of the BOTB Study Group in 1979 is still not getting through nearly a decade later: many firms appear still not to recognise the value of language training or acknowledge that languages are an important factor in export success. The firms that do try to use the foreign language in their dealings with overseas customers are still heavily dependent on language agencies for translation and local agents for advice

Secondly, there is the optimistic view: from our professional point of view, the results of the questionnaires are quite heartening, since we have here an untapped market for the employment of those who complete our College's business–orientated courses in the major European languages.

Obviously there are further exciting possibilities for Higher Education establishments who are prepared to meet the challenge of the other languages such as Japanese and Russian and offer *ab initio* courses to students and businessmen alike. The results of the survey should provide justification for any institute of Higher Education to stop hesitating and get involved in providing foreign languages to the local business community. Employees trained appropriately in Higher Education are a powerful asset to any business involved in exports; not only do they have a high level of linguistic expertise, but their awareness of the culture of the countries involved is a vital factor in successful exporting. They are, of course, able to contribute to the firm over a wide range of commercial activities on a non–language basis.

The comments from firms ranged from the personal anecdote to the *cri de coeur*: "I am attending a private language school in Edinburgh, studying Spanish... I have found the knowledge attained to date to be useful in business... I was required to attend contract negotiations in

Madrid last September and there was no doubt that the ability to converse... in Spanish was a decided advantage and did influence the attitude of our client"; and "What British export needs is dynamic, hard–working numerate industrialists capable of communicating in three languages, English and two others"; or, "knowledge and respect for the other man's culture win a lot of battles".

So there is hope... but the onus is on education to encourage local firms, firstly, to accept that there is a need for some foreign language expertise then positively to discriminate in favour of hiring staff who have a viable level of foreign language competence. In the immediate, the local Higher Education establishment should provide appropriate in–house courses and language learning packages. If industry and education work together, we will be well on our way to restoring languages to its rightful place in our education system, gaining recognition for their long neglected place in the hierarchy of necessary management skills and, finally, promoting a better and more commercially rewarding image for the British exporter.

References and Notes

1   *Survey of exports from Scotland in 1984* Scottish Council for Development and Industry.

2   *Foreign Languages for Overseas Trade* (1979) Report of the British Overseas Trade Board.

APPENDIX A

1 With which of the following countries/ groups of countries does your firms deal in the course of its overseas trade? (Indicate order of importance)	2 With which of these countries does your firm deal in English? (Please tick)	3 How large is your firm's involvement in the use of the Foreign Language? (Ring letter)
Arabic–speaking ☐	☐	S F O I N
French–speaking ☐	☐	S F O I N
German–speaking ☐	☐	S F O I N
Italy ☐	☐	S F O I N
Japan ☐	☐	S F O I N
Portuguese ☐	☐	S F O I N
Spanish ☐	☐	S F O I N
USSR ☐	☐	S F O I N

Key: S = substantial, F = frequent, O = occasional, I = infrequent, N = nil.

4 For which purposes does your firm require the following skills in the Foreign Language?

(Please indicate order of importance)

5 How are these needs met at present?

(Please ring letter)

(a) Spoken:
personal contact
with customers in
their own country   OA FE LA PC OM

interpreting for visitors to this
country   OA FE LA PC OM

(b) Written:

translation into
the Foreign Language   OA FE LA PC OM

translation from
the Foreign Language   OA FE LA PC OM

Other

Key: OA = overseas agent; FE = your firm's own employees;
         LA = language services agency; PC = personal contacts;
         OM = other means

6   What are the main areas of linguistic expertise involved? Please
     indicate order of importance:Commercial/Technical/
     Legal/Marketing/ Other

7   How many employees are there in your firm. Please tick.
     1 to 50   51 to 500   over 500

Chapter 5

THE USE OF FOREIGN LANGUAGES IN EAST MIDLANDS INDUSTRY AND COMMERCE
David Hind and Brian Hollis

Industrial Profile of the East Midlands[1]

In most of the region, as in the rest of the United Kingdom, construction and service industries employ between half and three quarters of the work-force, with mining and manufacture accounting for most of the remainder. A dominant feature of the industrial profile of the East Midlands is the highly productive coalfield on both sides of the Nottinghamshire/Derbyshire border and extending southwards into Leicestershire. However, the associated iron and steel industry has now considerably declined in the area.

As demonstrated by the breakdown of firms making positive responses to the questionnaire, the companies involved in export trade fall mainly into the following categories: textiles/clothing/footwear, chemicals/pharmaceuticals, mechanical/electrical engineering and electronics. The textile industry, represented mainly by hosiery or knitwear manufacture, has two kinds of location: large towns or cities (Leicester, Nottingham, Loughborough), together with neighbouring villages, and the coalfield, where it provides female employment to complement mining. The city of Leicester, where nearly 25% of the region's textile workers are concentrated, also includes a substantial amount of footwear manufacture.

The chemical industry, ranging from cosmetics and pharmaceuticals to heavy industrial chemicals is also prominent in the region. The light end of the industry predominates in the East Midlands, with Boots of Nottingham by far the largest centre, whereas the heavy end of the industry, although less important in the region, is found mainly on the coalfield, particularly in Chesterfield.

About 60% of the region's electrical and electronic engineering is shared fairly equally between Nottingham, Loughborough and Leicester, whereas light mechanical engineering, another important export sector, is distributed evenly through Nottinghamshire,

Leicestershire and Derbyshire with outposts also in mainly rural Lincolnshire. The manufacture of transport equipment other than motor vechicles is particularly strongly represented in the Derby and Nottingham conurbations.

Finally, food, drink and tobacco companies are distributed throughout the region, ranging from a major employer in Nottingham to firms processing agricultural products in rural areas, particularly Lincolnshire.[2]

Analysis of the Survey [3]

Over 700 firms in the East Midlands were sent questionnaires. Replies were received from 120, of which 15 were rejected as not being suitable for the survey. The main criterion on which the selection was based was the extent to which the respondent showed an interest in the use of foreign languages, rather than simply whether the firm had foreign contacts through exporting and/or importing. In a few cases, although there was no such trading activity, responses to Questions 4,5 or 6 indicated that the firm either made some use of languages or could possibly do so in the future. Thus all figures in this survey are based on a sample of the 105 firms which justified inclusion on these grounds.

Of these firms the most common category mentioned (see Q.3 in Appendix 1) was mechanical engineering (category 7), but in fact most of the firms which indicated that the export/imports came under category 8 (electrical engineering) were also included in category 7. Therefore, for the purposes of this survey these two categories have been put together, making a total of 28 individual firms. Apart from "Others", of which there were 20 , the other most common categories were textiles, clothing, footwear, in which there were 16 firms, chemicals, fine chemicals, pharmaceuticals with 10 firms, electronics with 6 firms, and miscellaneous manufacture with 6 firms.

Trade Profile of Responding Companies

Answers to Question 1 on exports revealed that 90 out of the 105 firms in the sample were exporting to non–English–speaking countries, and that the size of these exports as a proportion of their total company sales ranged from 1% to 90%. For most firms, however, the proportion was under 50%, although a very respectable 36% of firms were exporting over a quarter of their products to countries where they might expect to need languages other than English.

Table 2, which illustrates similar details of foreign imports into the East Midlands, showed a similar total range between 1% and 100% for the 72 firms involved in purchases from non–English–speaking countries. However, a comparison of Tables 1 and 2 shows a very positive balance of trade, since such imports were far less significant than the exports – only 15% of firms purchased more than a quarter of their needs from these sources, compared with the achievement of 36% of firms which exported more than a quarter of their needs from these sources, compared with the achievement of 36% of firms which exported more than a quarter of their products to non–English–speaking countries.

Table 3 provides a rank order of languages used by firms, whether by their own staff or by agents, in actual export deals. As confirmed by later tables, Western Europe is by far the most important export market for firms in this region, with German (27%) leading French (24%) as the language most frequently used, and other European languages following some way behind (e.g. Spanish 8%, Italian 8%, Scandinavian 7%). The importance of markets in the Near and Far East is underlined by the fact that 7% of transactions were conducted in Arabic and 6% in Oriental languages including Chinese. These relatively low percentages for Arabic and Chinese in actual use compare significantly with perceived lost opportunities for exports illustrated by Table 4 (Arabic 14%, Chinese 9%), and potential areas of trade growth revealed by Table 5 (China 18%, Middle East 11%).

The Language Need

The next issue to be examined was that of language 'need', as specified in Questions 4 and 7. As can be seen from the answers to Question 4, 41% of the firms felt that they could have significantly improved their trade performance over the last few years if they had had more access to foreign language facilities. The European languages feature largely in the responses, but others, namely Japanese with 15%, Arabic with 14% and Russian with 12% figure fairly significantly. Replies to Question 7, which assumes a 'need' where firms have bought in the services of an outside translating/interpreting bureau within the U.K. or abroad in the last three years or so, indicate that 41% of firms have not done so, while 57% have used the services of bureaux in the U.K. and 10% commissioned those abroad. 27% of the firms replied 'no' to both questions. As can be seen the spread of languages is very much the same as for Question 4, with German and French and Spanish heading the list. In some cases firms mentioned the same language in answers to both these questions, again the most common being German (9), French (8) and Spanish (4).

Of the categories which are of particular interest in this survey engineering firms showed the greatest need for language services, with 23 firms, of which 8 responded to both Questions 4 and 7. Perhaps more significantly, 11 of the firms in category 12 (i.e. out of a total of 16) felt they could have more export success with greater use of foreign languages. Thus it can be seen that the need is only answered to some extent by the use of translating services. 35% of the firms were seen to have a 'need' in their response to both questions.

Activities of Foreign Language Use

The principal activities where the companies have used a foreign language in trade contacts (Question 6) fall into three distinct categories. The first involved reading letters and telexes (62%), using the 'phone (52%), writing letters and notes (51%) and travelling abroad (51%). When it is taken into account that 14% of the companies did not respond at all to this question, these figures represent a very high percentage of the respondents. The second category involved reading technical or sales literature (33%), 'social chat' (29%) and writing trade documents (27%). It is perhaps surprising to find that the second activity mentioned here figures in a relatively low position as one might well have expected that the 'wining and dining' side of language use would have seemed to be more significant to many firms.

Giving talks (8%) or listening to talks (6%) ranked as low priorities for these firms, whereas among the 'other activities' (9%) mention was made of using languages for quotations, exhibitions, videos, listening to reading, operating manuals, selling abroad, negotiations and commercial discussions. It can be assumed that some of these activities could well have been seen by other companies as being included in one of the activities specifically mentioned.

Opportunity was given to the respondents to indicate which activities they thought were of particular importance. Travelling abroad (14%) and reading letters etc. (13%) headed the list here, while writing trade documents produced a similar response to using the 'phone and writing letters.

When one looks at specific company–types certain differences do appear in comparison to the general picture outlined above. In the engineering sectors (firms in Categories 7 and 8) the only figure which differs to any degree is that of 'reading technical literature' (47%), which is not particularly surprising. Although the sample for categories 4 and 5 is small, (10 in all, and 9 responded to this question) there is a clearer commitment to the use of languages in their own categories. There is a use well above the average in travelling abroad (8 firms), using the 'phone (6 firms), writing letters (6), and reading technical literature (7).

There were 15 responses to Question 6 from companies in the textile, clothing and footwear area, and these, too, showed an increase over the average in some activities – social chat (8 firms), travelling abroad (9), using the 'phone (12) writing letters (12). It is possible that these firms feel the need for greater activity in the export field if they are to survive. It is quite clear from the response to this question that there is considerable use made of foreign languages by firms, and that in some company–types more emphasis is put on them than others. What has not been ascertained by this survey is to what extent and at what level in the company this use is made. There is a need for future research here. It is also clear that companies which display a language need in other parts of this survey in fact make use of languages in some areas of their activities.

It can only be assumed at this stage that when it comes to negotiating and selling many companies do not have the necessary expertise at the right level. They can cope with the everyday activities, but at the sharp end, as it were, of business they depend on the use of language bureaux or resort to the use of English.

Survey of Specific Transactions with Foreign Companies

An analysis of answers in Table 3 reveals that in the 65 export accounts where the foreign language was used, the size of deal ranged from £10,000 to £10 million p.a., and that the grand total value of these exports from the East Midlands was £60,864,000. 17 export accounts of over £1 million p.a. were recorded where the foreign language was used in negotiations; in these cases French, German, Arabic and Oriental languages received three mentions each, Spanish two, and European, Scandinavian and Italian one mention each.

The languages used in export negotiations (in terms of languages mentioned, regardless of size of deal) were: German (19), French (17), Spanish (6), Italian (6), Arabic (5), Scandinavian (5), Portuguese (3), Various European (3), Dutch (2), Oriental (2), Chinese (2), and Russian (1). A comparison with answers to Question 4 indicates, perhaps surprisingly, that firms are more confident of their own or their agents' ability to negotiate in German, and see a slightly greater need for an improvement in French coverage. However, the relatively low use made of Oriental languages (no mention of Japanese!) as compared with the need for Japanese and Chinese as indicated in the table for Question 4 is an obvious argument for increased availability of these languages to export firms in the region. Out of 105 responding firms, 52% used local agents in their export negotiations. However, some firms were active in more than one country or region, and when one takes into account the 275 separate export deals recorded, the proportion of those in which agents were used rises slightly to 54%. In 32% of the export deals recorded, English is **not** given as the language of transaction, although the fact that this column is often left blank where an agent is used suggests that the actual percentage of deals negotiated in the foreign language may be much higher.

A further comparison of the responses to Questions 7 and 8 shows that 28 companies using outside language agencies also indicate that they have some in-house expertise. These covered the full range of languages, with 15 mentions of German and 12 of French. It is also possible to ascertain whether companies use their own staff or not when exporting by comparing the responses to Questions 3 and 8. 48 companies indicated they had some in-house expertise (with 73 language-mentions). In 20 cases they used a local English agent and the business was conducted in English; in 32 cases a local agent was using his own language. Where the company's own staff was used, 16 used English and 20 the local language. This gives support to the conclusion which was drawn from the study of responses to Question 6, that a large number of firms do not, or are unable, to make use of the language skills of their own staff when working in the export field.

As compared with present usage of foreign languages for export (Question 3), answers to Question 5 point firstly to the potential markets in the Far East, including China, and to a lesser extent, Japan. However, there remains a discrepancy between the figure of only 4% of firms seeing an increased need for Chinese (Question 4) and 18% viewing China as a potential area for trade growth (Question 5). Similarly, only 5 firms had used Arabic for export negotiations (total value £5 million), only 6% felt that they would have improve their trade performance with access to Arabic, but 11% see the Middle East as an area of potential trade growth. By contrast with the earlier North of England surveys, France has a very slight edge over Germany as a perceived potential growth area for firms in the East Midlands.

Conclusions

From the survey made in the East Midlands area it can be seen that:-

1. Many firms are interested in the use of languages in their business as seen by their response to this questionnaire;

2. There are definitely perceived language needs in that firms feel they could export more given greater access to language skills;

3. Where these skills exist within a firm they may be suitable for everyday use but in many cases are not exploited for work in foreign markets;

4. German and French are seen as being of roughly equal status when it comes to language use and language need;

5. There is a definite interest in languages outside the European area, particularly Arabic, Chinese and Japanese;

6. Institutions at all levels of education where languages are presently taught need to rethink the range of languages they offer in line with those required by industry and commerce to-day and incorporate an appropriate balance of skills into their teaching programmes.

APPENDIX A
TABLES 1-8: RESULTS of the EAST MIDLANDS SURVEY

TABLE 1

Question 1: Sample of firms: 105

Exports to non-English-speaking countries as a percentage of total
company sales

	No. of firms	Percentage of sample
75 - 100%	3	3%
50 - 74%	8	8%
25 - 49%	26	25%
1 - 24%	53	50%
0%	15	14%

TABLE 2

Question 2: Sample of firms: 105

Imports from non-English-speaking countries as a percentage of
total company purchases

	No. of firms	Percentage of sample
75 - 100%	4	4%
50 - 74%	4	4%
25 - 49%	7	7%
1 - 24%	57	54%
0%	33	31%

TABLE 3

Question 3: Sample: 71 export transactions

Languages used in export transactions (other than English)

1.	German	27%	7.	Portuguese	4%
2.	French	24%	8.	Various European	4%
3.	Spanish	8%	9.	Dutch	3%
4.	Italian	8%	10.	Oriental	3%
5.	Arabic	7%	11.	Chinese	3%
6.	Scandinavian	7%	12.	Russian	1%

TABLE 4

Question 4:   Sample of firms: 105

Do you feel there are any countries/regions where you would have significantly improved your trade performance over the last few years with access to foreign language facilities?

No	59%
Yes	41%

If so, which languages?

Sample: 43 Positive Respondents   %Total Sample

N=43			N=105
1. 56%	French	(23%)
2. 42%	German	(17%)
3. 35%	Spanish	(14%)
4. 19%	Japanese	(8%)
5. 14%	Italian	(5%)
6. 14%	Arabic	(5%)
7. 12%	Russian	(5%)
8. 9%	Chinese	(4%)
9. 9%	Scandinavian	(4%)

TABLE 5

Question 5:   Sample of firms: 105

Which non–english–speaking countries do you consider potential areas of trade growth for your company over the next few years?

1. 85%	West Europe		11. 7%	Japan
2. 34%	Far East		12. 6%	Netherlands
3. 18%	China		13. 5%	Belgium
4. 17%	France		14. 5%	USSR
5. 17%	Spain		15. 4%	N. Africa
6. 16%	Germany		16. 4%	Portugal
7. 11%	Middle East		17. 3%	Scandinavia
8. 11%	E. Europe		18. 2%	India
9. 10%	N. and S. America		19. 2%	Switzerland
10. 9%	Italy			1% each:

Bulgaria, Czechoslovakia,Denmark, Pakistan, Poland

TABLE 6

Question 6: Sample of firms: 105 (Response Rate – 86%)

Principal activities where companies have used a foreign language in trade contacts with foreign companies:

1.	Reading letters/telex	62%
2.	Using the phone	52%
3.	Travelling abroad	51%
4.	Writing letters/notes	51%
5.	Reading technical/sales lit.	33%
6.	Wining and dining (social chat)	29%
7.	Writing trade documents	27%
8.	Miscellaneous (quotations, exhibitions, etc.)	9%
9.	Giving talks/speeches	8%
10.	Listening to talks	6%

TABLE 7

Question 7:   Sample of firms: 105

Have you bought in the services of an outside translation/interpreting bureau here or abroad during the past 3 or so years?

Yes, here	57%
Yes, abroad	10%
No	41%

If 'yes', for which languages?

Sample: 62 Positive Respondents

German 30%
French 25%
Spanish 17%
Arabic 15%
Italian 11%
Chinese 10%
Russian 5%
Japanese 4%
Czech 1%
Korean 1%
Polish 1%

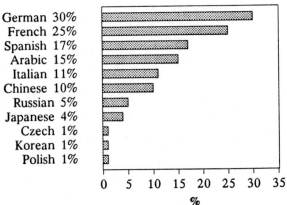

%

TABLE 8

Question 8:   Sample of firms: 105

For which Languages have you used your own staff (or Head Office) for foreign contacts over the past 3 or so years?

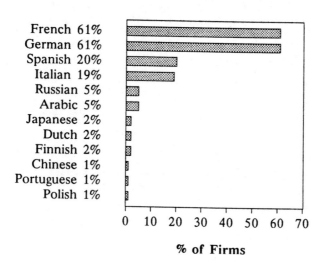

French 61%
German 61%
Spanish 20%
Italian 19%
Russian 5%
Arabic 5%
Japanese 2%
Dutch 2%
Finnish 2%
Chinese 1%
Portuguese 1%
Polish 1%

0   10   20   30   40   50   60   70

% of Firms

References and Notes

1. The Counties of Derbyshire, Nottinghamshire, Leicestershire and Lincolnshire.

2. With acknowledgements to: R. Hammond (1985) 'The East Midlands in Maps 7 – Industrial Employment 1981' IN: *Trent Geographer* No. 5.

3. All Tables and Questions referred to appear in Appendix A at the end of this chapter.

Chapter 6

FOREIGN LANGUAGES IN THE INDUSTRY OF OXFORDSHIRE AND THE THAMES VALLEY
Marilyn Farr

"We find our language ability gives us a competitive edge over other UK exporters"- *the words of a precision engineering company responding to questions about the use of foreign languages in industry.*

The questionnaire[1] devised by Steve Hagen for his survey of foreign language use in industry in the North-East of England was used in Oxfordshire and the Thames Valley on two occasions in 1986 and 1987. Firstly, in Spring 1986 Abingdon College of FE distributed questionnaires to companies with whom it had contact in its immediate area. There were 60 respondents of which 28 are classed as positive responses; ie where the companies concerned were engaged in export and/or import activity. The questionnaire was then used by the Oxford LX Centre (LEXIS) in May 1987. A list of 423 companies in Oxfordshire, Berkshire and the Swindon areas of Wiltshire was compiled from various sources. Sixty-three completed questionnaires were received; of these, 60 were positive responses. For the purposes of this study the two sets of responses were analysed together, giving 88 in all.

The respondents to the survey are trading across a very wide range of sectors. Of the 17 industrial classes listed in Q3 only mining is not mentioned by companies. The category "other" is most frequently cited, with some 23 areas of trade from books to engineering software. Otherwise, for both imports and exports, the largest categories are *mechanical engineering, electronics* and *electrical engineering*, with a large group of companies engaged in *instrument/precision engineering* represented amongst exporters.

Of the 88 respondents, slightly over three quarters (77%) export to non-English speaking countries. For the overwhelming majority of these (87%), such exports represent under 40% of the goods/services sold, with more than half of the companies achieving less than 20% of their sales in non-English speaking countries. The picture for exports to English-speaking countries is not very different, although a higher proportion of companies do have sales to these countries of 40–60% of their total.

Overall, a relatively small proportion of goods and services is bought from abroad by the respondents. The majority of importing companies in this sample obtain less than 20% of goods and services from imports (58% of those importing from non-English speaking and 88% of those importing from English-speaking countries.) The 12% of companies who import 90–100% of goods/services stand out as being for the most part subsidiaries of foreign companies or distributors whose principle trading activity is to import finished manufactured goods (vehicles, furniture, cosmetics, electronics) from one or two sources for sale in this country.

In the case of both exports and imports it is difficult to translate the levels of trading activity indicated above into cash terms, as many companies did not provide details of the value of goods bought and sold. There was a similar reluctance to divulge annual turnover, but from the 35 companies who did provide this information it is possible to deduce that we are dealing with companies from the very small to the very large. Figures quoted ranged from £250,000 to £100 million, with about two thirds of companies below the £5 million mark.

The range of countries with whom the companies in our sample trade is very large. No fewer than 65 countries and regions were given, some of which overlapped (eg 'the Mediterranean', 'Western Europe', 'the EEC'), providing something of a nightmare when it came to analysing the results. What was quite clear, however, is the importance of the EEC as a trading partner; 59% of exporters mentioned at least one EEC country, many listing several, and EEC countries were mentioned by 49% of importers. The only other countries or regions mentioned a significant number of times were Scandinavia, the Middle East and Japan. Tables 1 and 2 indicate the individual countries most frequently mentioned. The importance for our sample of West Germany alongside France as an export customer will be noted, as well as its predominance as a source of imports.

Table 1. Major export markets (N = 76 exporting companies)

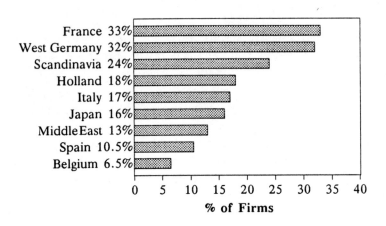

Table 2. Major sources of imports (N = 77 importing companies)

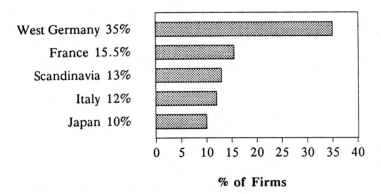

For the foreign language teacher much of the interesting information to be gleaned from Q3 has to do with the language used in transactions. The comment: "Fortunately for us the international language for electronics is English", was unique in our sample. Table 3 brings together countries/regions speaking a common language and indicates the language of transactions in those countries, in so far as this information was provided.

Table 3.   Use of languages in export transactions

Countries speaking:	No. of companies carrying out transactions in:		
	FL only	Eng only	FL and/or Eng
French	15	9	2
German	8	13	6
Spanish	4	3	2
Portuguese	2	3	–
Italian	2	6	2
Japanese	1	7	3
Chinese	2	1	–

French is clearly the preferred language in French–speaking countries. A further breakdown of the figures shows that this is particularly true of France itself (French:English in the proportion 2:1), whereas English is much more acceptable to Belgian companies. In dealings with West Germany, English alone is used twice as frequently by the companies in our sample as German alone. The samples for the other language areas are unfortunately rather small, but the use of English in transactions with Italy and Japan stands out clearly. In Q3 the use of language presumably focusses on the negotiation of a deal, letters, contracts, etc and may not reflect the use of language in the social intercourse which surrounds the actual negotiation, and in which even a modest attempt to address a business partner, in his/her own language may have a positive effect on the outcome of the deal.

Tables 4 and 5 give full details of the frequency with which each of the languages listed was used in export and import transactions respectively. The relative importance of French and German in these tables clearly relates to the relative importance of France and West Germany in exports and imports as indicated Tables 1 and 2.

Table 4.   Exports – Language of Transactions

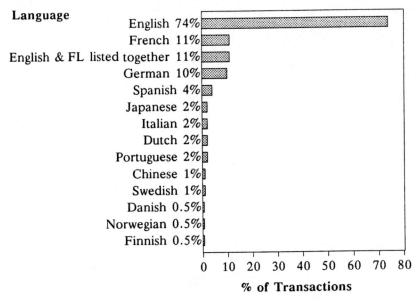

(N=186 i.e. No. of instances in which
the language of transaction is given)

Table 5. Imports – Language of Transaction

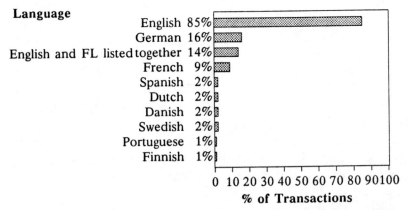

(N=87 i.e. No. of instances which
the language of transaction is given)

There may be some ambiguity in the information available to us in
answer to Q3. Approximately 50% of English–only transactions

involved the use of a local agent or interpreter, whereas this was so for only about 30% of foreign–language–only transactions. The respondent trading in a foreign market through an English–speaking agent may well class the language of such transactions as English. If he goes into that market directly he might come up against the need to use the foreign language; whereas the agent probably acts as a buffer against such problems. We can only speculate on this, and on the greater potential for his business if he were to go into the foreign market as a speaker of the language.

One would perhaps have expected a local agent or interpreter to be used more frequently in those cases where the language of the transaction is the foreign language only. In fact, in 31 cases of transactions in the foreign language where no agent was used, the companies concerned were apparently able to draw on the foreign language capabilities of their own staff, as indicated by their responses to Q8, in all but 5 instances.

Table 6.   Use of FL compared with Use of Agent

No. of transactions using:		Agent used: No. of companies	%
FL only	45	14	31
English only	107	52	48.5
FL and/or English	21	16	76
No information about language	32	19	59

However, particularly disturbing is the proportion of companies apparently failing to perform adequately for lack of foreign languages. A little under half of the companies surveyed (43%) believed they *could have improved their trade performance* with access to better foreign language facilities. Of the languages needed Spanish and Italian were seen as being as important as German, with most other languages, except perhaps Japanese, much less significant.

Foreign Languages In The Industry
Of Oxfordshire And The Thames Valley

Table 7.   Rank Order of Languages with Potential for Improving Trade Performance

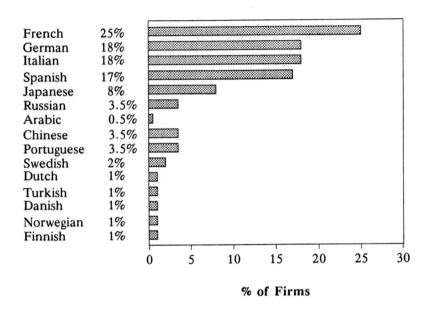

French	25%
German	18%
Italian	18%
Spanish	17%
Japanese	8%
Russian	3.5%
Arabic	0.5%
Chinese	3.5%
Portuguese	3.5%
Swedish	2%
Dutch	1%
Turkish	1%
Danish	1%
Norwegian	1%
Finnish	1%

% of Firms

Further evidence of need is apparent in the reliance on outside language agencies. 52% of the total sample said they had bought in language services, mostly in this country (Q7). If we put together the information from Q4 and Q7 we find that the number of respondents answering 'yes' to either question or both gives us an overall picture of where foreign language expertise in companies is lacking, leading either to business opportunities not being taken up or to business having to be supported by the buying in of expertise. No fewer than 63.5% of companies responded with 'yes' to one or both of these questions. This suggests that there is a considerable market for the provision of both foreign language training for companies and other foreign language services, such as translation. In the list of languages for which translation and interpreting services have been bought in, Arabic and Russian make a slightly more significant, though still small, showing compared with elsewhere in the survey. Japanese again appears, significantly on a par with Russian.

Table 8   **Rank Order of Languages for which Services Bought in**

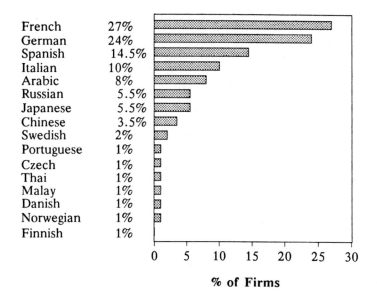

French	27%
German	24%
Spanish	14.5%
Italian	10%
Arabic	8%
Russian	5.5%
Japanese	5.5%
Chinese	3.5%
Swedish	2%
Portuguese	1%
Czech	1%
Thai	1%
Malay	1%
Danish	1%
Norwegian	1%
Finnish	1%

% of Firms

The responses to Q8 show that approximately three quarters of companies (74%) have used the foreign language skills of their own staff in recent years. Table 9 gives details of the relative importance of the various languages. We have seen earlier in the analysis that the need for German in business is consistently high – comparable with the need for French. As Table 9 shows, despite its lack of prominence in the school curriculum, German is not far behind French as a skill that can be called on by companies. Given the information gleaned about export markets it is not perhaps surprising to find the need for Italian is ahead of Spanish (see Table 1). It is perhaps surprising, however, that 28% of companies have staff who have skills in one or other of these languages (22% Italian, 20% Spanish), again given their lowly status in schools, though not, it should be said, in adult education. The experience over many years of Oxford College of FE for example, is that evening class enrolments for German, Spanish and Italian at Beginners, O and A levels, are not far behind those for French. Many students also cite the need for the language in their work as one of their reasons for learning that language.

Table 9. **Rank Order of Languages for Which Companies Use Own Staff (N = 88)**

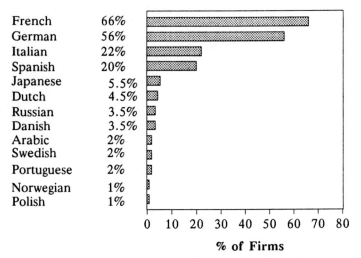

French	66%
German	56%
Italian	22%
Spanish	20%
Japanese	5.5%
Dutch	4.5%
Russian	3.5%
Danish	3.5%
Arabic	2%
Swedish	2%
Portuguese	2%
Norwegian	1%
Polish	1%

% of Firms

Combining the information of Tables 8 and 9 and counting each language only once for each company, gives us an overall picture of the use of foreign languages in industry in the Oxfordshire and Thames Valley area.

Table 10.   Rank Order of Languages for Which Companies Use Own or Agency Staff (N = 88)

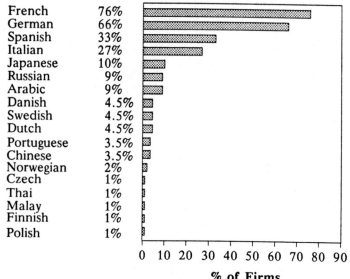

French	76%
German	66%
Spanish	33%
Italian	27%
Japanese	10%
Russian	9%
Arabic	9%
Danish	4.5%
Swedish	4.5%
Dutch	4.5%
Portuguese	3.5%
Chinese	3.5%
Norwegian	2%
Czech	1%
Thai	1%
Malay	1%
Finnish	1%
Polish	1%

% of Firms

Q6 concerns the principal activities in which companies use foreign languages in trade contacts. From the information requested, it is not possible to tell whether some activities are more important in one language than in another. But the information nevertheless provides useful indicators for the providers of foreign language training and producers of teaching materials as to what the main thrust of their work is likely to be.

Foreign Languages In The Industry
         Of Oxfordshire And The Thames Valley

Table 11.   Rank Order of Principal Activities
         (N = 70 i.e. No. of respondents giving information on
         this question)

Rank Order	Activities	All mentions (N=70)	%Total Sample (N=80)	Rated "most important" (rank order)	
1	Reading letters/telexes	80%	(63)	14%	(2)
2	Using the telephone	74%	(59)	21%	(1)
3	Travelling abroad	70%	(55)	13%	(3)
4	Writing letters/notes	54%	(43)	8.5%	(5)
5	Reading tech/sales lit	48.5%	(38)	8.5%	(5)
6	Wining and dining	47%	(37)	5.5%	(6)
7	Writing trade documents	37%	(29)	10%	(4)
8	Giving talks/speeches	21%	(17)	3%	(7)
9	Listening to talks	20%	(16)	–	

Others (added by respondents): Negotiations/Business
transactions 4%, Sales visits 3%, Exhibitions 3%, Writing
telexes, Contact *(sic)* & Tender documents, Description of
goods to electricians, Literature 1%

If these are grouped under the three headings *reading, writing* and
listening/speaking skills we can see that the latter category is mentioned
by far the greatest number of times, even if we concede that "travelling
abroad" could also be assigned to the category "reading" (reading of
signs, notices, timetables, etc). Reading is the next most important
category, and writing, to which traditional foreign language teaching
has given primacy, comes last. It is however significant to note that of
those who use the foreign language for writing trade documents, over a
quarter consider this to be "most important", thus placing this skill
fourth in the rank order of most important activities, whereas it is only
seventh in the overall rank order. It is at the same time the skill which
can be most easily bought in.

Table 12. Relative Importance of Reading, Writing and Listening/Speaking Activities

Activities (List No.)	No. of times mentioned
All reading activities (6, 8)	90
All writing activities (4, 5, telexes, tender)	66
All listening/speaking activities (1, 2, 3, 7, 9 + "other")	171

Finally, Q5 asked companies to look to the future, and indicate those non–English speaking countries which they see as potential growth areas for their own trade. As in the case of their actual trade to date, more companies are looking to the EEC, and especially to France and West Germany, than to any other area. Italy and Spain are close behind, but other EEC countries and other countries of Western Europe are little mentioned. Nor do many of the countries surveyed see opportunities in Eastern Europe. Next most important after the EEC, and roughly equal, are Japan, China, Scandinavia and the Middle East. South America is not seen by many as an area with potential by our respondents.

Foreign Languages In The Industry
Of Oxfordshire And The Thames Valley

Table 13. Potential Areas of Trade Growth (N = 88)

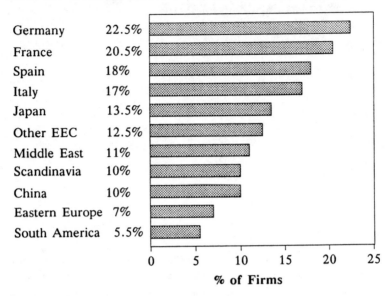

Germany	22.5%	
France	20.5%	
Spain	18%	
Italy	17%	
Japan	13.5%	
Other EEC	12.5%	
Middle East	11%	
Scandinavia	10%	
China	10%	
Eastern Europe	7%	
South America	5.5%	

% of Firms

Conclusions

The message of the survey in this area of Britain appears then to be that, as is becoming clear in other parts of the country too, the ability of people in industry and commerce to use German is as important as ability in French. Spanish and Italian also need to be accorded a much greater significance than as a nation we have traditionally granted them. Japanese is already needed (and used) by small but significant number of companies and this need is likely to grow if the above predictions about future trade growth are fulfilled. And even if much business in these countries continues to be done through the medium of English, one must not forget another area of knowledge not addressed by this survey, but of great importance for successful trading, namely knowledge of cultural differences, business practices in the foreign country, etc. Language teachers and successful exporters together surely have a role here in disseminating such knowledge.

While individual companies can demonstrate a good range of foreign language capability amongst their staff – one company listed eight languages – nearly half (43%) had used their own staff for French and/or German only , and only a third (34%) had used staff for any other language apart from French and German. This is not to say that there are not staff in these companies with languages they have not yet been called upon to use. However, more than half the companies using their own staff for French and/or German only indicated in their answers to Q4 and Q7 a need for other languages. In any case, staff move on to other jobs, and expertise in a given language may be lost to the company. Our survey would seem to show, on the whole, that there is a considerable gap between the foreign language needs of companies and what they can supply themselves. As one of our informants commented : "Of all the export salesmen I come into contact with I am unusual in being able to communicate in the foreign language".

Lack of foreign language expertise can be bad for business. As we have seen, almost half the companies surveyed felt that this factor held them back from improving their trade performance in certain countries. There is at least a suggestion, though the figures are too low to be statistically reliable, that companies that do business in the foreign language on average sell a higher value of goods than those who use only English.

Table 14.   Value of Exports Compared with Language of Transaction

Value £	No. of companies using FL only as lang. of transaction	No. of companies using Eng. only as lang. of transaction
Up to 50,000	1	33
51,000 – 150,000	4	8
151,000 – 500,000	3	11
501,000 – 1 million	1	4
Above £1 million	5	3

The task of bridging the gap between current language capabilities in companies and their present and future needs is not going to be an easy one. Apart from the problems, outside the scope of this study, of the place of foreign languages in Britain's schools and universities, there are plenty of difficulties for the foreign language teacher and her/his student in industry to contend with: problems of long-term planning, of the difficulty of selecting the right languages, of fitting language learning in amongst other professional commitments – to name just a few mentioned by our respondents. Nevertheless, industrialists and language teachers alike should perhaps bear in mind the words of the Managing Director of a tool-making company – a company now doing about £200,000 of business a year in the country in question : "We would not have made progress in France without the ability to communicate".

Acknowledgements

The carrying out of this survey was very much a team effort and there are more people to whom thanks are due than it is possible to mention here by name. We are most grateful to Steve Hagen for allowing his questionnaire to be used and for very helpful guidelines on its use and interpretation. Much hard work was done by Mike Bloom and his colleagues at Abingdon College of FE in carrying out the survey in their area. Members of the Steering Group of LEXIS gave much useful advice, and provided valuable help in compiling the list of companies, especially Anne Fitzsimons, CELP Co-ordinator, and Chris Allen, Chairman of the Oxford and District International Traders Association. Others who provided names of relevant companies were Helen Price of Slough College of HE, Mark Dodsworth of the Bath LX Centre and Celia Mackenzie-Price of the Oxford LLMI project. Thanks are due also to secretarial staff at Oxford College of FE, and finally to my colleagues in LEXIS – Jane Millar, for practical help, constructive comments and moral support, and Linda Ludlow, whose newly-learned word-processing skills were put to good use.

References and Notes

1.   See Appendix 1

Chapter 7

FOREIGN LANGUAGES IN INDUSTRY AND COMMERCE IN EAST ANGLIA
Maidi Brown

Introduction : Survey Rationale

The purpose of the survey was to find out in a more systematic way the extent of the need for foreign language services, and how this need is matched by existing skills among staff in the firms taking part in the study. The results of the survey were expected to help predict future needs, provide the firms themselves with a valuable needs analysis and shape the development of language courses at Essex Institute and other colleges in the region.

The firms taking part in the survey were selected at random from published registers. In the latter part of 1986 questionnaires were sent to a wide range of establishments from manufacturing firms to businesses in the services sector. Geographically, the area covered included counties in the East Anglia, but with a greater concentration on Essex – the most populated non-metropolitan county in England.

Historically, East Anglia had been a quiet backwater out of the mainstream of industrial development, still predominantly rural and agricultural in character, particularly north of the Cambridge–Ipswich areas. However, for the purposes of this survey, attention has focused on the southern part of the region where the picture is more urban, largely due to the proximity of the capital; i.e. centres like Southend with a large commuter population and new towns such as Harlow and Basildon, established in the 1950's and 1960's to accommodate London 'overspill', have since become industrial and commercial centre in their 'own right' alongside established industrial towns like Dagenham and Chelmsford.

The region has emerged into the 1980's with significant advantages to enable it to fulfil the role of a 'gateway to Europe':

a) It has a low proportion of declining heavy industries and a strong industrial base in buoyant areas such as electrical and electronic engineering (GEC–Marconi, STC, Plessey), vehicle building (Ford), chemicals (Bayer, Courtauld, Shell). This in turn has made the area an attractive location for new hi–tech firms setting up in the areas of electronics, precision engineering, pharmaceuticals and bio–chemistry. Service industries, particularly in the financial sector, are increasingly in evidence because of good communications and the presence of a suitably qualified workforce. The area also enjoys the advantage of being close to the services and markets of the London area and close to the Continent, facilitating export trade and attracting inward investment.

b) These locational advantages are backed up by an excellent transport and communications infrastructure. The region boasts the ports of Felixstowe – the biggest container port in the UK, Harwich – a container port of note and the biggest passenger port in the area and Tilbury – the third largest UK container port. The M11, M25 and improved A12 have opened up areas that might otherwise have been unattractive to investors, and the siting of the third London airport at Stansted should further open up the area to international traffic.

In short, the region has recently experienced the fastest growth of any U.K. region outside London and its environs is well placed in many ways to play a leading role in industrial and commercial expansion and in trade with Europe. The findings from the survey of this region are therefore invested with a particular significance.

Analysis of the Returns

A total of 428 questionnaires were sent out, of which 122 were returned, i.e. an above–average return of 28%. Moreover, the responses were made promptly and frequently accompanied by a covering letter or a telephone call expressing interest even from those who were not declared language users. Of the 122 enterprises who responded, 59 said they were using foreign languages in their business contacts with non–English speaking countries. We therefore retained these 59 responses as the sample (N = 59) on which to establish our findings.

The design aimed to facilitate answers and minimize inconvenience for respondents. However, in a number of cases questionnaires returned were inadequately filled in and contained either incomplete or approximate answers. Nevertheless, we did not feel that these shortcomings hindered our analysis to any significant extent. In some cases they provided us with some interesting anecdotal evidence. In actual fact the analysis yielded a great deal of data about the nature of the enterprises, the language services needed or used and the countries involved in business transactions.

A selection of data was made to provide evidence in four key areas which had been identified as significant for our research:

    (i)   the types of enterprises operating in the region
    (ii)   the recent use of foreign languages in transactions
    (iii) the expressed need for foreign language services
    (iv) the use of and need for specific languages and specific language skills

Profile of Enterprises

It is interesting to note that in an area experiencing rapid population growth, the manufacturing enterprises dominate in our survey. Our analysis showed that 69.5% of declared language users were in the manufacturing sector and 30.5% in the services sector. Both the traditional and new industries feature, but those involving new technologies dominated the field: 24% defined themselves as being in the 'electronics' industrial class, 19% in 'precision engineering' and 17% in 'mechanical engineering'.

No systematic pattern emerged which allowed us to relate the size of the enterprise to the use of foreign languages. Of the total sample 56% indicated the size of their turnover ranged from £0.3 million to £500 million. But, notably, all those companies with a turnover in excess of £100 million (11.9% of the total) had linguist staff available who provided services in more than 2 languages.

The volume of exchanges with non–English–speaking countries emerged as being very significant; 66% of enterprises purchased at least 25% of their goods or services from non–English–speaking countries, 67% of enterprises sold at least 25% of their goods or services to those countries.

Information Relating to Present Use of Foreign Languages in Trade and Industry

By analysing the responses of all manufacturing enterprises who either imported from or exported to non–English–speaking countries we found that 53% of companies conducted the transaction in the local language and 63% of these companies resorted to the services of a local agent or an interpreter abroad.

These results indicate therefore that only 37% of companies had the necessary staff to transact in the appropriate foreign languages, which is confirmed when the responses from the total sample are considered; ie 59% of enterprises had recently bought in the services of an outside translation/interpreting bureau.

However, when the purpose of language use was less specific, ie only "foreign contacts over the past 3 years," rather than actual completed transactions, the proportion of companies using their own staff becomes far more significant with 83% of the total number of enterprises reported having used their own staff for foreign contacts.

The complexity of the field is apparent when examining the use of foreign languages, which covers a very wide spectrum of language activities ranging from making a simple telephone inquiry to translating a highly specialized technical document. Depending on the scope of their activities different enterprises will require different skills, in different languages, at various levels, which we shall examine in greater detail later.

An Analysis of the Use and Need for Specific Languages and Language Skills

In the questionnaire four questions aimed to obtain data relating to the specific languages used, or needed, in the region: (1) in–house language use; (2) reliance on outside agencies; (3) underperformance due to lack of languages; (4) use of languages other than English in transactions:

Fig. 1:   IN–HOUSE LANGUAGE USE

In Fig. 1 (N=59) the chart shows the percentage of companies in which staff used their languages for foreign contacts:

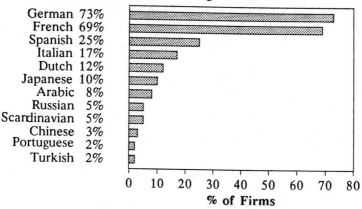

Language	%
German	73%
French	69%
Spanish	25%
Italian	17%
Dutch	12%
Japanese	10%
Arabic	8%
Russian	5%
Scardinavian	5%
Chinese	3%
Portuguese	2%
Turkish	2%

% of Firms

Fig. 2:   USE OF OUTSIDE LANGUAGE AGENCIES

The chart in Fig. 2 (N=59) shows the percentage of companies which used outside translation/interpreting bureau for specific languages:

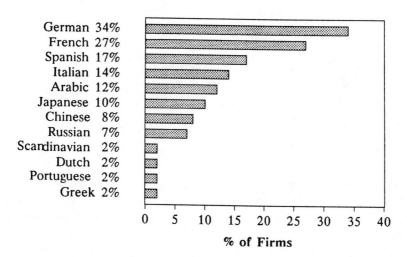

Language	%
German	34%
French	27%
Spanish	17%
Italian	14%
Arabic	12%
Japanese	10%
Chinese	8%
Russian	7%
Scardinavian	2%
Dutch	2%
Portuguese	2%
Greek	2%

% of Firms

Figures 1 and 2 point to a clear lead by the major European languages. Over 50% of Britian's commercial exchanges are with EEC countries; German is slightly ahead of French, and there is the very significant presence of Middle and Far Eastern languages; Arabic, Japanese and Chinese. Companies using both their own staff and outside agencies for any one language are worth singling out as a category with extensive language needs. Of the 48 companies which had made use of their own staff for foreign contacts, 22 had also had to have recourse to a translation/interpreting bureau in the same language. In 37% of such cases the language was German and in 25% French. This relatively high percentage in the two most common languages reveals the limitations of staff who may not be skilled in the more demanding language activities such as technical translation or interpreting.

Our inquiry into the loss of trade due to lack of foreign languages indicates that 26 companies were in need (44%) and the languages needed are broken down in Figure 3 (N=59):

Fig 3: FOREIGN LANGUAGES NEEDED

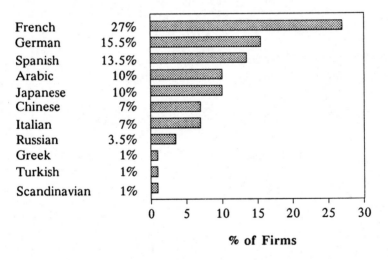

French	27%
German	15.5%
Spanish	13.5%
Arabic	10%
Japanese	10%
Chinese	7%
Italian	7%
Russian	3.5%
Greek	1%
Turkish	1%
Scandinavian	1%

% of Firms

A surprisingly larger number of companies named French as their problem rather than German. Yet, as shown in Fig. 2, far more companies approached outside agencies for help with German than did for French! The answer to this apparent contradiction must remain speculative but it could be suggested that companies are more willing to "muddle through" in French, which appears less technically forbidding than German and which more English people have experience of, than with German where staff might accept their limitations more readily. In addition, French businesses frequently offer greater resistance to the use of English in their contacts and may insist on French being used – certainly, when buying. This hypothesis is borne out by the results shown in Figure 4.

French appears very clearly as the language most used when the *transactions actually completed* were conducted in a language other than English. Clearly companies relying on staff equipped with just "school French", be it 'O' level or 'A'level, would have difficulty in meeting the requirements. There is clearly a need for staff who are specially trained in the skills required by industry and commerce.

**Fig. 4: TRANSACTIONS COMPLETED IN FOREIGN
LANGUAGES OTHER THAN IN ENGLISH**

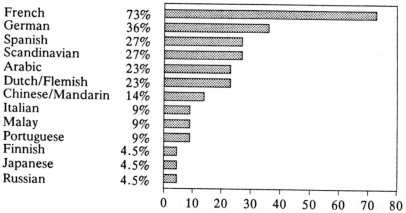

French	73%
German	36%
Spanish	27%
Scandinavian	27%
Arabic	23%
Dutch/Flemish	23%
Chinese/Mandarin	14%
Italian	9%
Malay	9%
Portuguese	9%
Finnish	4.5%
Japanese	4.5%
Russian	4.5%

A comment made by one leading company highlights some of the difficulties: "We have never found it too difficult to get access to Foreign Language facilities, both in the UK or abroad, when we needed them. In our Industry most of the language of transaction is English, occasionally papers need to be translated. However, we often have an uneasy feeling that if our staff who meet foreign customers could converse in their language, as they all can in English, we could develop better relations that could help in getting more business".

In terms of evaluating a possible core content for training programmes the principal language activites used in foreign trade contacts are:

Fig 5: SKILLS REQUIRED BY COMPANIES

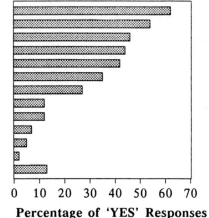

Language Activity

Reading Letters/Telex
Travel Abroad
Reading Tech/Sales Lit
Using the Phone
Entertaining Business Contacts
Writing Letters/Notes
Writing Trade Documents
Listening to Talks
Giving Talks/Speeches
Sales
Formal Meetings
Interpretation of Documentation
Nil Response

0 10 20 30 40 50 60 70

Percentage of 'YES' Responses

Sectoral Analysis: Foreign Language Needs And Training Solutions

At the heart of our inquiry into foreign language needs was the issue of whether companies could have improved their trade performance significantly over the last few years with access to foreign language facilities. A sizeable proportion of our sample (44%) indicated this to be the case. Moreover, the overwhelming majority (84%) were companies in the manufacturing sector, indicating the 'foreign language factor' had a role to play in their fortunes. The results showed very clearly the vulnerable position of manufacturing companies in world trade: 78% of companies in the manufacturing sector saw their future prospects dependent on trade links with non–English–speaking countries, compared with 44% of companies in the services sector.

Upon analysis, the companies' in–house policies revealed that out of our total sample only 32% had a policy which took knowledge of a foreign language into account when recruiting staff. Within this sample those belonging to the services sector represented just 27% of that sector while those belonging to the manufacturing sector represented 34% of that sector. Moreover, companies' language training policies produced even less impressive figures. Only 13% of our total sample claimed they had such a policy. We found that only 16% of service enterprises considered it worthwhile to offer training to their own staff while a disappointing 12% did so in the manufacturing sector. In fact, only 9.7% of manufacturing enterprises and 11% of service enterprises admitted to having both a foreign language training policy and a language orientated recruitment policy. In terms of the departments, over 50% of these companies indicated that marketing/export was the area where languages were a definite asset. Sales and contracts were given by 36% and "technical" by 15%. Even on a such a limited sample these are clear indications that the most "useful" linguists are those who combine language skills with a broad business background.

These findings show the companies' responses to be at best inadequate and at worst catastrophic in view of the fact that 67% of our total sample see non–English–speaking countries as potential areas of trade growth. In many cases it seems companies consider that buying in foreign language services is the option that serves them best – indicated by the 59% who had bought in outside language services. Not surprisingly, the need was greatest for the manufacturing enterprises who made up 82% of that figure.

Significantly, 50% of the companies that had recourse to outside translation/interpreting services also stated that their trade performance would have been improved with access to facilities *in the same language*. This apparent contradiction confirms a definite mismatch between needs as they are perceived and the services available. Similarly, 33% of the companies using their own staff also admitted to loss of trade because of lack of access to facilities *in the same language*. Moreover 45% of the companies which had made use of their own staff for foreign contacts had also had to have recourse to an outside agency *in the same language*. The implications of this finding is clear – even where the linguistic needs are perceived, enterprises are having difficulty in matching their needs with the appropriate foreign language facilities in the appropriate languages. There is no doubt that to a certain extent this must be due to the very wide range of language skills that are required (see Fig.5) and the large number of languages – 12 or so – commonly in use by companies:

When compared with other surveys such as Hagen's Northern Survey or the LCCI Survey, one very striking discrepancy feature emerges. While 'reading letters or telexes' and 'travelling abroad' occupy the same prominent place in all three surveys, *reading technical and sales literature* appears in third place in this survey, having been quoted by 46 enterprises as one of the principal language activites used. This, however, may not be unrelated to the fact that 50% of all the manufacturing companies in our sample described themselves as being in the engineering sector, either 'electronic', 'precision' or 'mechanical'. High priority should therefore be given to the receptive reading skills which involve processing information received in the foreign language in order to make it accessible in English. Also of prime importance are the productive speaking skills in well-defined areas which involve social skills as well: travel abroad, using the phone and entertaining business contacts.

Fig 6:   **PROSPECTS FOR FUTURE TRADE**

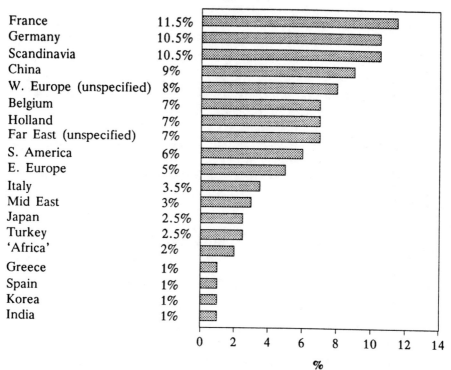

France	11.5%
Germany	10.5%
Scandinavia	10.5%
China	9%
W. Europe (unspecified)	8%
Belgium	7%
Holland	7%
Far East (unspecified)	7%
S. America	6%
E. Europe	5%
Italy	3.5%
Mid East	3%
Japan	2.5%
Turkey	2.5%
'Africa'	2%
Greece	1%
Spain	1%
Korea	1%
India	1%

%
Expressed as a percentage of the
total frequency response for these areas

Future needs as shown in Figure 6 will continue to call on the languages spoken by Britain's immediate neighbours, as well as requiring a willingness on the part of young linguists and business people to tackle Oriental languages from scratch. In recent years 40% of language graduates leaving university have failed to find initial employment where their language skills are made use of; if more of these students had combined courses in languages with business, management or sciences, the country at large, as well as the graduates themselves, could have benefited substantially from the additional dimension of knowledge.

Chapter 8

FOREIGN LANGUAGE NEEDS OF SOUTH-EAST FIRMS
Professor C Cobb

From the early 1960's onwards, roughly coinciding with Britain's first, unsuccessful, attempt to join the Common Market, there has been a fairly constant expression of concern over the inadequacies of the national provision for modern languages training and the negative influence that this could have on Britain's export effort. But, whilst the argument appeared totally convincing, the provision has, in fact seriously declined. More recently, at ministerial level, there have been clear statements of determination to reverse the trend, both from Kenneth Baker and Angela Rumbold.

There are, of course, many noteworthy cases of firms setting up excellent in-house services to make good these deficiencies, but there are big variations in practice and part of the difficulty arises from a lack of information about the real nature and extent of the problem. The survey by Hagen at Newcastle Polytechnic served as the basis for a regional study carried out by Kingston Polytechnic with specific reference to South East England.

In all there were 77 responses to the questionnaire* and their geographical distribution corresponds roughly to the area served by the Kingston Regional Management Centre.

Table 1: **Location of the Firms participating**

London, West and South West	26%
Surrey	15%
London Airport Area (Uxbridge, Hounslow)	12%
Kingston	10%
Crawley (Gatwick Airport Area)	10%
Central London	10%
Kent	4%
East Sussex	3%
Other (Berks, Bucks, Hants, Herts)	10%

*14 of these did not consider that their activities were covered by the questionnaire, 8 were incomplete and 3 were importers only.

Table 2: Industrial Classification of Firms

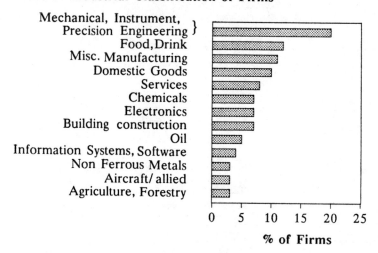

As might be expected, the spread of activities in Table 2 is very great. At one end of the scale the firms in the mechanical, instrument and precision engineering sector represent a well-established tradition in the vicinity of the London Airports, whilst, at the other, one would expect to find a considerable group of firms in the service industries (Food, Drink, Consultancy Services, Information Technology).

Table 3: Percentage of Firms (grouped by industrial classification) exporting more than 20% of their goods and services to non-English speaking countries

Chemicals	100%
Aircraft, allied	100%
Information Systems, Software	100%
Non Ferrous Metals	100%
Electronics	75%
Oil	66%
Mechanical, Precision and Industrial Engineering	65%
Misc manufacturing	60%
Food, Drink	40%
Domestic Goods	33%
Services	20%

The questionnaire was designed to concentrate on firms with a considerable activity in the export field and, in order to underline this point, those devoting a sizeable part of their efforts to exporting to the non–English speaking world have been highlighted.

Clear differences begin to emerge and it is significant that many of the firms in the service industries concentrate on trading in the local region.

Table 4:   Area to which exports are directed
(Percentage of firms listed in Table 3 directing exports to these areas)

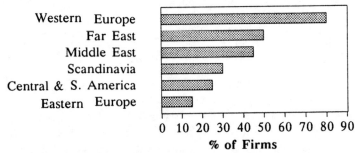

This table contains no surprises but it is more interesting to read it in conjunction with the responses concerning areas in the non–English speaking world considered to have a potential for trade growth. (The answers here refer to all respondents and not simply those listed in Table 3)

Table 5:   Percentage of Firms indicating future increased export potential in the following areas

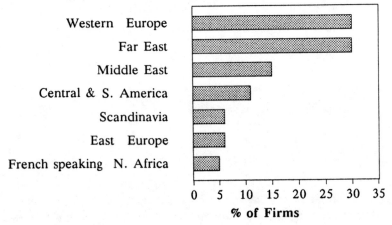

It is clear that although Western Europe is easily the most favoured market amongst British exporters, a considerable number of firms still see it as an area with a potential for growth in exports. Whilst the percentage of those at present trading in the Middle and Far East are roughly equal, it is interesting to note that prospects in the Far East are seen in a considerably more optimistic light (16% of all firms listed China as a possibility). For the future, Central and South America are seen as an almost equally attractive prospect as the Middle East.

The responses up to this point provide a basis of factual information concerning the types of firms, their location and activities in the export field. The remainder of the questionnaire refers more precisely to the central theme under examination : the use of foreign languages as part of the sales drive.

Table 6: **The Provision of Foreign Language Skills Within Firms : Percentage of Firms using their own in-house language skills (N=52):**

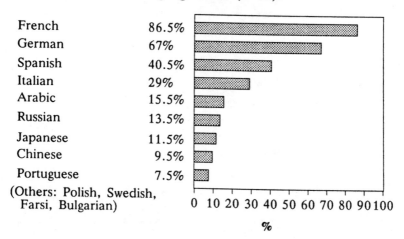

French	86.5%	
German	67%	
Spanish	40.5%	
Italian	29%	
Arabic	15.5%	
Russian	13.5%	
Japanese	11.5%	
Chinese	9.5%	
Portuguese	7.5%	

(Others: Polish, Swedish, Farsi, Bulgarian)

0 10 20 30 40 50 60 70 80 90 100

%

N.B. The responses should not be taken to mean that the firms can cope with all their needs in these languages : many have in addition required the services of outside translating and interpreting agencies.

The clear predominance of French is a reflection of the unequal provision of modern language teaching in British schools. Nevertheless the figures for all other languages are higher than the percentages studying these languages at secondary level and this in itself is an interesting reflection of how British Industry has had to strive to go some way to righting this illogical imbalance. Despite this one should not overlook the fact that 25% of the 52 foreign–language–using firms stated that *they could have significantly improved their trade* over the last few years if they had had access to foreign language facilities in these languages:

Given the importance of the Middle and Far Eastern markets it would be interesting to know more about the type of provision which has been made for acquiring linguistic skills and the ways in which this can be improved and extended. Almost certainly a fair number of the Japanese, Chinese and Arabic speakers employed by firms will be natives of those countries, but given the expansion of trade foreseen this can be no more than a stop–gap measure.

Table 7:   Languages needed where companies 'could have significantly improved' trade (N=13)

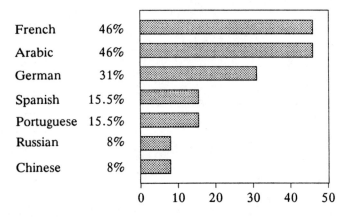

French	46%
Arabic	46%
German	31%
Spanish	15.5%
Portuguese	15.5%
Russian	8%
Chinese	8%

Percentage 'Yes' Response

Beyond these generalities it is more interesting to look in detail at the wide variations of practice and provision within firms. When faced by the complacent comment that all business with foreign clients is conducted in English, it is illuminating to go to the other end of the scale and take an outstanding example of good practice : Pharos Marine of Brentford. Significantly (and perhaps worryingly) the firm is a subsidiary of the Swedish company Pharos AB of Stockholm. The

London manager, Mr Bo Terling, comments that they sell all over the world and are used to handling any language. Their staff can cover the following languages : French, German, Spanish, Russian, Italian, Portuguese, Polish, Farsi (and, of course, Swedish). Indonesian is the only language where they had to bring in outside assistance. Equally noteworthy is the very active use made of these languages. This is by no means confined to travelling and social uses or the reading of trade literature. Particular importance is given to daily phone contacts and, in addition, foreign language skills are mentioned as being important for the writing of trade documents and for giving talks and speeches abroad.

Total perfection is utopian. A major concern like ICI have staff to cover French, German, Spanish, Russian, Italian and Portuguese, together with very clear ideas of how these skills are used : to the usual list they write in "Business negotiation" and "After-sales service". Nevertheless, such is the scale of their operations that they have had to call in outside assistance in Greek, the Scandinavian languages, Turkish, Polish, Romanian and Serbo-Croat.

A good example of a keen awareness of what is involved is provided by Babcock Power where their own staff can cover French, German, Spanish and Russian, specifically pointing to a need to undertake business discussion, both technical and commercial, in the foreign language. They note that they could have significantly improved their trade performance over the last few years if they had had access to foreign language facilities in Arabic and Chinese and they point to China, Iran and Iraq as potential areas of trade growth.

BCAL conduct large operations with France, Germany and the Middle East with all the transactions taking place in the foreign language without their being obliged to make use of outside assistance. In similar fashion the Aylesbury firm, Rexel Ltd., a member of the Ofrex Group, use their own staff to conduct business in the foreign language with France, Germany, Italy and Latin America. Narrowing down the market, BOC conduct all their business with France and Germany in French and German and see both countries as areas for potential trade growth.

If these are cases of using the more accessible West European languages there are firms who, despite all the difficulties, can cope with a range of more remote languages. Thus, VG Scientific of East Grinstead have staff familiar with Russian, Japanese, Chinese, Bulgarian and Polish.

Many other cases of good practice could be listed but a particular example of all round awareness of the problem is provided by Beecham Products Overseas. They have an in-house language service and their own staff can cover in French, German, Spanish, Portuguese, Arabic and Japanese. In addition to the more normal activities carried out in the foreign language (daily contacts, perusal of trade and sales literature), they specifically mention the need to converse with distributors and local traders (retailers and wholesalers). There is, however, no complacency in their approach and they note that they could have improved their trade performance if they had had increased access to foreign language facilities in Arabic, Russian and Spanish. With such an approach to foreign trade it is not altogether surprising that they show a keen eye for future, potential markets, listing Spain, Italy, Angola and Hungary.

Significantly, there were many instances in which those firms with the most developed back-up in foreign languages also showed a sharper perception of their specific requirements. Examples like "negotiation", "technical and commercial discussion", "after-sales services" or "discussions with overseas distributors" have already been mentioned. The Chemical firm, Troxide, with considerable exports to Germany, South America, Japan and the Far East and staff capable of covering French, German, Spanish, Italian, Portuguese, Cantonese and Japanese also add "face to face discussions" to the list of situations where the use of a foreign language has been found necessary.

There is no easy separating line between firms with extensive facilities and those without : demand frequently outstrips supply as is evidenced by a speciality metals firms exporting to Western Europe and the Far East, with staff able to use French, German, Italian, Japanese and Chinese to conduct sales negotiations and yet still needing to make use of translating/interpreting agencies both in Britain and abroad for French, German, Japanese and Chinese.

Foreign Language Needs of Firms

One good measure of foreign language needs is, of course, the degree of reliance on outside language agencies such as translation bureaux. Out of the 52 exporting companies in the survey 32 indicated using an agency over a range of 16 languages. German and Arabic are particularly prominent, whilst demand for Chinese and Japanese is bouyant (see Table 8).

Table 8: Buying-in of Outside Language Services (N=52)

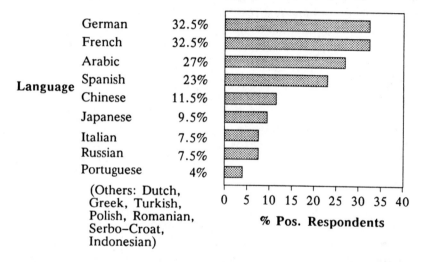

Language		
German	32.5%	
French	32.5%	
Arabic	27%	
Spanish	23%	
Chinese	11.5%	
Japanese	9.5%	
Italian	7.5%	
Russian	7.5%	
Portuguese	4%	

(Others: Dutch, Greek, Turkish, Polish, Romanian, Serbo-Croat, Indonesian)

% Pos. Respondents

There are, nevertheless, indications of a less than enthusiastic approach to foreign markets : a construction firm whose only venture had been to the Middle East reported gloomily that they had "no plans to work abroad again". More than one firm relying entirely on the services of specialised agencies referred loosely to the use of "local languages", rather like native patois. Certain firms (for example in the petrochemical field) can claim with some justice that English has become the international language of the industry. Nevertheless, the contrast with other countries is frequently brought out in the references to imports : a timber firm has no problems in finding suppliers in Russia, Poland, Czechoslavakia, Sweden and Finland ready to use English to promote their sales.

Many of these firms give few indications as to the activities in which foreign languages might be used and are equally sparse in their references to potential new markets. Other organisations have taken great strides towards anticipating future change and responding to the need for language training. A fascinating example of a complete change of policy is provided by the Agricultural Training Board who report, "The Agricultural Training Board is expanding its overseas activities and this will mean moving away from British colonial areas which are still, basically, English speaking. We are completing a survey within our own staff to find out the range of overseas languages available to us and there is at the present time a realisation at agricultural colleges that it would be very helpful, in terms of future employment, for students to be able to continue a foreign language alongside their agricultural courses". They point to potential markets in French speaking Africa, South America and the Middle East and note that they are held back by the lack of access to foreign language facilities.

There is a fair amount of evidence to support the claim that the smaller firms will have more difficulty in developing this type of linguistic coverage, but it is by no means an absolute rule. Gomsall Tanneries export to Italy, Germany and Israel and have staff who can cover in French, German, Spanish and Italian. They do go on to note, however, that they could have improved their performance in the French and German markets with access to more extensive foreign language facilities. But the more usual situation is that of the smaller firm already involved in exporting, conscious of additional potential markets, with only access to limited foreign language facilities and aware of the way in which this is hindering their performance.

Examples:-

- A firm specialising in Information Technology can only provide cover in German and Italian but hopes to extend its operations to the whole of Western Europe.

- A Mitcham firm trading in France and Spain has only access to facilities in French.

- A specialist glass manufacturer sees the whole of Western Europe as a potential market but can only cover French and German.

- An Instrument manufacturer can cover activities in French,

German and Russian but is aware that performance is being hindered through lack of facilities in Chinese and cannot cover for future markets in the Middle East and South America.

- A firm specialising in Transportation Equipment has only French and German speakers but has a big operation in the Far East and hopes to expand into Eastern Europe.

- A Guildford firm can only cover French (and even that inadequately) but also trades in the Middle and Far East which it sees as areas of potential expansion.

Conclusions

Despite the size of sample, a number of interesting findings on companies in the South East are worth highlighting:

1. There seems to be wider in-house coverage of the more exotic languages, like Arabic, Japanese and Chinese, than in other parts of Britain, which is probably due to greater availability of native speakers around London;

2. Even companies with well-developed language support services have admitted they could perform better with more language facilities;

3. As a general rule, the smaller company which has poor in-house coverage of languages with only limited penetration of the export market appears to be in greatest need of foreign language facilities;

4. Admission of underperformance due to lack of language facilities appears lower than in other samples in Britain, but 25% of the sample still represents major lost opportunities;

5. Policy and practice on foreign languages can vary greatly between different companies; much depends upon the degree of enlightenment and forward planning amongst the management of firms.

Chapter 9

FOREIGN LANGUAGE USE IN SOUTH HAMPSHIRE
Bob French

Introduction

The questionnaire drawn up by Steve Hagen of Newcastle Polytechnic was distributed to members of S.E. Hampshire Chamber of Commerce and the Chichester & District Chamber of Commerce and also to industrial and commercial firms in Hampshire contacted through the Dorset Institute of Higher Education and the Southampton Institute of Higher Education, together with a further sample provided by the S.E. Hants Committee for Industry Year.

The original intention was to limit the investigation to Southern Hampshire, including the two largest cities in S.E. England outside London (Southampton and Portsmouth), however, it also became possible to include the Chichester area, so in effect the survey covers the coastal strip from Lymington in the West and across the boundary into W. Sussex as far as Bognor in the East, extending inland as far as Ringwood, Winchester and Horndean. The only replies received from outside this area were therefore where local firms had passed the questionnaire on to their head office. There was quite an even spread of response with two peaks for Portsmouth and Southampton, as might be expected.

The categories of the questionnaire which was originally prepared for the N.E. of England were not totally suited to an area with no coal or heavy metal industries. Shipbuilding, railway and motor vehicle industries are of course still represented but clearly the dominant feature in terms of the number of firms involved is in the category of electronics, information technology, tele-communications, defence and pharmaceuticals. The very nature of some of the work involved and the competitiveness of rapidly developing areas meant that some firms were reluctant to give any of the details asked for in the questionnaire because the information requested "is of a sensitive nature" or "is not released as a matter of company policy".

Of the 62 replies received nine came from firms who were 100% home market companies, firms of accountants or "UK Builders only", three were from a multinational using "English as a lingua franca world wide", two from companies with large defence contracts naturally unwilling to disclose information and one from a part of the IBA who found the questionnaire "not really applicable", which continued, "however, we do have European contacts and run and support French and German language training". The analysis of responses is consequently based on the remaining 47 firms which provided details of their use (or non–use) of foreign languages in their deals with non–English speaking countries.

The Use of Foreign Languages across Regional Trade

An examination of the type of goods and services exported by the firms which responded fits in well with the overall spread of industries in the area: mechanical engineering, miscellaneous manufacturing, marine engineering, electronics and services. The highest percentages of trade with non–English speaking countries (50%) were reported by one firm specialising in dress–making patterns and another in heating and ventilation. Both made wide use of local languages.

In response to the part of the questionnaire designed to elicit latent needs, 46.8% felt there were countries where they could have significantly improved trade performance over the last few years if they had had access to foreign language facilities. The languages which it was though could have contributed to improved performance are indicated in Table 1.

Table 1   **RANK ORDERING OF LANGUAGES IN TERMS OF NEED (N = 47)**

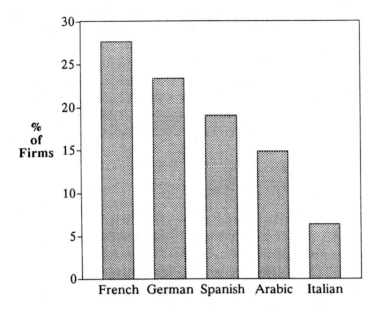

Also mentioned: Korean, Malay, Russian

The comparative weighting of these unmet needs correlates closely with the general European orientation of trade and the potential areas of growth envisaged.

Of course, this is not a measure of the perception by the responding companies of the usefulness of foreign languages to their business since, although 25 (53.2%) answered 'no' or did not reply to this question, only four (8.5%) of these had not felt a need for, or already made use of, foreign language skills; only 2% to 5% of their business was in exports and this with Scandinavia and Holland. Even the high-tech firm which stated, "They all speak the language of technology – English" had made use of employees' expertise in French, Spanish and Portuguese. The comment is eloquent proof of the underlying complacency prompted by the feeling that the other person will always understand English.

The European Community accounts for the vast majority of the trade with non-English speaking countries and is mentioned by 90% of the respondents, the second most frequently mentioned market being the Middle East (34.8%). The perceived *potential* for trade growth with non-English speaking countries again reveals a natural orientation towards Western Europe as shown in Table 2.

Table 2   AREAS FOR POTENTIAL FUTURE TRADE GROWTH

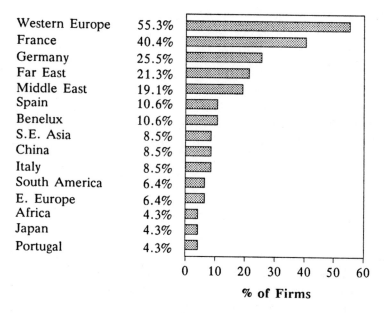

Western Europe	55.3%
France	40.4%
Germany	25.5%
Far East	21.3%
Middle East	19.1%
Spain	10.6%
Benelux	10.6%
S.E. Asia	8.5%
China	8.5%
Italy	8.5%
South America	6.4%
E. Europe	6.4%
Africa	4.3%
Japan	4.3%
Portugal	4.3%

% of Firms

Also mentioned: Indonesia, Korea, Scandinavia, Turkey

It is useful at this point to compare the predictions with recent performance as set out in Table 3. Only the Far East shows a high percentage positive difference between actual achievement and perceived potential. As one respondent put it "those are very competitive markets". Whether or not they thought they had lost trade through a lack of access to language facilities, the proportions having bought in the services of an outside translating or interpreting bureau were very similar. Taking the whole group, 55.3% had bought in translation services in the UK and 12.8% had used a foreign-based bureau. 32.6% had not made any use of bought-in translation services. However, of that third of the sample only two firms (4.3%) had not had language services provided by their own staff. These were the firms trading in English only with Holland and Scandinavia for 5% or less of their trade.

Table 3   MAJOR MARKETS IN 1983–1986

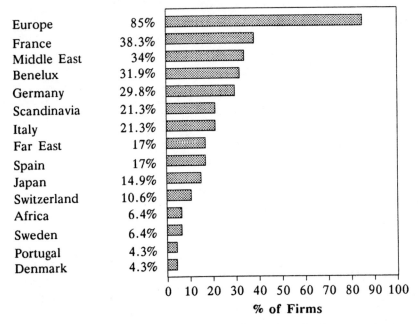

Europe	85%
France	38.3%
Middle East	34%
Benelux	31.9%
Germany	29.8%
Scandinavia	21.3%
Italy	21.3%
Far East	17%
Spain	17%
Japan	14.9%
Switzerland	10.6%
Africa	6.4%
Sweden	6.4%
Portugal	4.3%
Denmark	4.3%

% of Firms

The languages for which services had been bought in over the past three years once again (see Table 4) confirm the European orientation of the majority of firms. French and German clearly dominate with German running a very close second and after that a significant gap and considerable variation in the languages required.

**Table 4   TRANSLATION/INTERPRETING SERVICES
          BOUGHT IN (N=47)**

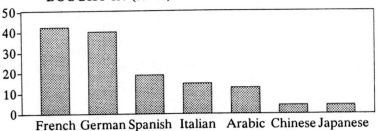

Also mentioned: Serbo–Croat, Thai

The use of own staff expertise in the same was 85.1% and covered a range of 13 different languages. Once again, the European domination is clear, see Table 5.

Table 5   IN–HOUSE EXPERTISE (N = 47)

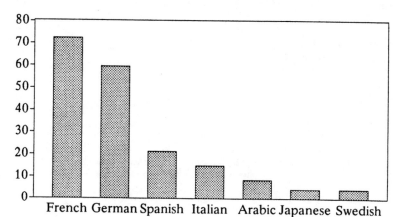

Also mentioned: Chinese, Dutch, Greek, Norwegian, Portuguese, Turkish

It is not surprising that linguistic ability in French is generally available within companies, considering how widely it is taught. Rather more noteworthy is the fact that almost 60% of these companies make use of a knowledge of German among their staff, which tends to weaken the general assumption that since our major competitors are so good at English we do not need to learn their language.

To obtain a complete picture of the range of languages used over the last three years in local industry and commerce, the data behind tables 3 and 4 were re-examined and combined with each language, counted only once per company. The resulting picture is set out in Table 6.

The resulting high position of German should once again be noted and also the fact that more than one third of the companies had had occasion to use Spanish. In addition, there is a far from insignificant requirement for Italian, with over a quarter of the respondents mentioning its use.

Table 6   RANGE OF LANGUAGES USED (N = 47)

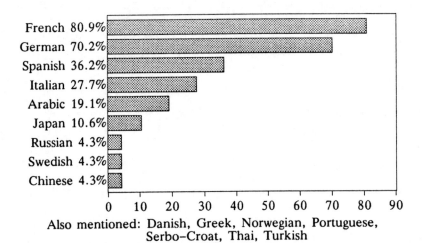

Also mentioned: Danish, Greek, Norwegian, Portuguese,
Serbo–Croat, Thai, Turkish

Firms found considerable difficulties in fitting in to the various
categories of product areas suggested and many resorted to the "Other,
please specify" category. From the information given, therefore, there
does not seem to be any real variation in the profile of trading for
which European Community languages are used. The main difference
between the products dealt with in these languages and those for which
Arabic was employed was the absence of the food/drink/tobacco
category and a greater emphasis on the services category for those
companies reporting the use of Arabic.

The most frequently mentioned use was 'travelling' (29), followed by
'reading letters/telex' (23), both of which are really inescapable for
anyone seriously engaged in trade with non–English speaking
countries. The order of skills and the other uses is shown in table 7.

These data would suggest that, although the traders concerned operate
orally at the individual, social level, they have little inclination to
participate in conferences and similar formal gatherings.

Table 7   FOREIGN LANGUAGE SKILLS IN USE

Key
▨ No. of firms
▨ % of sample (N=47)

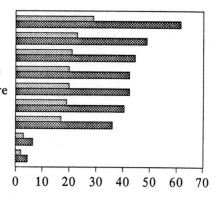

Travelling
Reading letters/telex
Telephone
Wining & Dining (social chat)
Rading technical/sales literature
Writing letters/notes
Writing trade documents
Giving talks/speeches
Listening to talks

0   10   20   30   40   50   60   70

It is perhaps worth noting the implied importance of oral skills which can be deduced from these responses. Totalling the oral skills categories, i.e. 'social chat', 'travelling', 'telephone' and 'listening to and giving talks', together with 'direct selling', 'technical discussions' and 'exhibitions', which were all listed against 'other (please specify)', there is a ratio of 82:79 oral to written skills. Clearly emphasising the importance of an ability to speak the language in addition to a reading knowledge. Furthermore the telephone situation is one where it is difficult to envisage buying in expertise.

Conclusion

Whilst the sample included here is too small to permit any general conclusions to be drawn, the findings seem to reinforce those of similar surveys carried out in other regions.

Acknowledgements

I would like to thank Mr E W Scovell of S.E. Hampshire Chamber of Commerce and Mr E Ellis of Chichester and District Chamber of Commerce for agreeing to distribute the questionnaires to their members, Doug Powell of Highbury College of Technology and Barbara Bishop of Southampton Institute of Higher Education for their assistance in contacting firms and organisations. I would address a special word of thanks to Mr T Tidd who made a selection of "likely" firms from the Industry Year Committee's mailing list and also to Mr H Barnett of the Hampshire Development Association for background information on the region. My thanks too to Steve Hagen of Newcastle Polytechnic for devising and supplying the questionnaire and generously advising on how to administer and interpret it. The shortcomings of presentation are entirely my own.

Chapter 10

FOREIGN LANGUAGES IN THE INDUSTRY AND COMMERCE OF THE FAR SOUTH WEST
D. Meacher, C.F. Hunns

Main Findings:

1) 43% of the firms in the sample could have performed better with languages;

2) French and German are the region's major languages needed, with Japanese, Spanish, Italian and Arabic close behind;

3) Language skills are most commonly used for travelling abroad and reading foreign correspondence and telex;

4) The sectors in greatest need are electronics and miscellaneous manufacture, followed by food/drink, engineering and textile industries.

5) EEC countries offer the greatest potential for future trade; especially Germany, France, Spain and Italy.

Origins

It seemed fitting in Industry Year to ascertain the foreign language needs of firms in the far South West of England, extending east down the peninsula as far as the city of Exeter. The questionnaire, devised by Stephen Hagen at Newcastle Polytechnic, was sent to some 200 firms and produced 37 meaningful returns, which formed the basic sample for the survey.

The Far South West: Industrial Profile

The far South West comprises the two counties of Devon and Cornwall, which, following the demise of tin mining and the decline of tourism, has become particularly depressed with unemployment rates in excess of 20%. In Plymouth, the major city of the two counties, the run–down of the dockyard has been a serious cause for concern, for, despite the relocation of many branch plants (often North American owned) to the region, defence–related industry is a major employer, accounting for around 25% of jobs.

Taken as a whole Devon and Cornwall are highly dependent on agriculture, fishing, tourism and the mining of china clay. The largest private sector employer is English China Clays, exporting clay through parts such as Fowey. As for agriculture there are exports and imports via the roll–on roll–off ferries between Plymouth and Roscoff and Plymouth and Santander. Fish and shell–fish are also exported through these outlets.

Profile of Sample

Two–thirds of our sample of 37 respondents conduct over three–quarters of their business in the UK. Taking 20% of a company's business operations to be a significant proportion of its activities, our analysis indicated that just under one–third of the positive respondents were engaged in at least that degree of selling to non–English speaking countries. On the buying side the figure is just under one–quarter of the firms. In our sample export and import trade with other English–speaking countries is only one–quarter and one–half as significant respectively, as that with non–English speaking countries. This suggests that our sample reflects the greater concern with non–English speaking markets now apparent in Britain's international trade pattern.

Evidence of Need

Nearly half our sample (43%) answered 'Yes' to the question, 'Do you feel there are any countries/regions where you could have significantly improved your trade performance over the last few years with access to foreign language facilities?' The main languages needed were German (19%), French (19%), Spanish (16%), Italian (16%), Japanese (16%), Arabic (13%), Russian (2%) and Chinese (2%).

When 'need' is expressed in terms of dependence on the services of an outside translation/interpreting bureau, a clear majority (57%) had resorted to outside services, but only here in the UK, none at all has done so abroad. As for the previous question, the listing in descending order is significant: French and German come first equal again, Italian second, Spanish and Arabic third, then Japanese and Dutch, with Russian eighth.

A comparison of Question 4 with Question 7 (23 respondents) reveals that: of the firms which considered that access to foreign language facilities would have enabled them to significantly improve their trade performance over the last few years:

13 firms felt that they could have done better, but tried (56.52%)
7   "   "   "   " could not have done better, but tried (30.43%)
3   "   "   "   " could have done better but didn't try (13.04%)

Industrial/Commercial Profile of Firms in Need

Of the 13 firms who answered 'Yes' to Q.4 (ie they felt they could have done better) and 'Yes' to Q.7 (ie they tried by enlisting language services), the sectors in descending order of mention are:

1. electronics and miscellaneous manufacture
2. food, drink, tobacco/mechnical eng./electrical
   eng./textiles, clothing, footwear.
3. agriculture & forestry, mining, chemicals and allied,
   ferrous metals, domestic goods and services.

The 33% of respondents in the S.W. who indicated that 20% or more of their activity was exporting to non–English speaking countries represented £230m of business in the financial year 1984–85. Against that, the 13 firms who felt they could have done better but tried had a turnover (1984–85) of £62.4m plus. The three companies which felt unable to divulge this information could have been quite substantial. Therefore language services could have **significantly** increased this global turnover of £62.4m. The potential gain in trade is not calculable, but could be staggering.

Significantly, 22 firms used their own staff in foreign contacts, and 86% of these did so for German, 77% for French, 27% each for Italian and Spanish, nearly 14% for Arabic and 4% each for Dutch, Japanese, Russian and Swedish. Of the 17 firms which used their own staff for French–speaking contacts, 5 felt that better language facilities could have significantly improved their performance, ie **29.41%**. The figures for the other languages were ; German 31.58% Italian 33.33%, Arabic 66.67%, whereas the firms were more satisfied with their in-house abilities in Russian, Spanish, Japanese.

The Languages in Use

Companies in certain sectors (see Table 1) are using a wider range of languages than those in other sectors. As one might expect, virtually every sector uses English to some degree for overseas trade. However, electrical engineering companies in our sample indicated use of four foreign languages (German, French, Roumanian and Polish). Firms in other engineering sectors used at least two foreign languages on average: electronics/communications and instrument/precision engineering made use of French, German and Italian, while two mechanical engineering companies indicated they had used Arabic and Turkish. Companies in the agriculture/forestry sector indicated use of Chinese, Arabic and German. Although English can be dominant at particular stages of the business activity, a number of companies have clearly grasped the need to operate in foreign languages.

TABLE 1: SPREAD OF LANGUAGES USED IN SPECIFIC TRANSACTIONS BY SECTOR AND VALUE

Description of Goods	Volume/Currency Exchanged	Languages (s) of Transaction
fine chemicals/ pharmaceuticals	£17 000K	English
electronics/lighting/ communications	£15 936K	Eng.Ger.Fr.
electrical engineering	£8 425.2K	Eng.Fr.Rum. Ger. Pol.
heavy engineering	£7 770K	English
mechanical engineering	£4 629K	Eng. Arab. Turk.
instrument/precision engineering	£3 000K	Eng. Ger. Fr. It.
food/drink/tobacco	£2 080K	–
Agriculture/forestry	£ 758.4K	Eng. Ger. Arab. Chin.

A pattern of skill use also emerged with companies indicating that 'travelling abroad' and 'reading letters and telex' were the most widespread activities where languages were used. The order of preference after these two was: 'wining and dining (social chat)', 'using the phone', 'writing letters/notes' and 'reading technical/sales leterature','writing trade documents', 'listening to talks' and 'giving speeches'.

It is interesting to point out that there is variation in skill use between sectors; electronics companies, for example, selected the order: 1. Using the telephone, 2. Writing trade documents, 3. Reading letters/telex , 4. Reading technical sales literature. On the other hand, electrical/ mechanical engineering firms preferred: 1. Travelling abroad, 2. Using the telephone, 3. Writing letters/notes, 4. Wining & dining etc. At the same time, food/drink/tobacco companies selected 'writing letters and notes' and 'travelling abroad' before the rest.

When companies were asked to give particular prominence to one skill or activity (an 'intensity rating'), 'travelling' came out as a top priority. Processing incoming letters or telex ranks almost as high, parallelled by use of the telephone. Nearly half the firms regarded the latter as their principal means of contacting clients abroad and 70% of those firms rated it as **the** most important means.

Principal Trading Areas

Table 2 indicates the frequency of contact of local companies by sector in the sample for given language areas where outside language services are engaged. It is significant that West Germany is most frequently cited, followed by Scandinavia. This brings into question not only the rationale for treating German as a minority language in our schools, but raises doubts over the need for languages in an overseas region where most British companies would expect to use English – Scandinavia.

Half the companies who responded to the question on trends in future trade indicated, first, Germany, followed by France, Spain, Italy, the Middle East, China, Far East, Eastern Europe, Japan, Russia, Benelux and Latin America. If we compare the responses to Questions 5 and 8,

the order of languages worth investing in is: French, German, Spanish,
Italian and Arabic.

TABLE 2: PRINCIPAL TRADING AREAS WHERE
COMPANIES DEPEND ON OUTSIDE LANGUAGE
SERVICES

Frequency	Country/Area	Extent Of Business	Class Of Business
******	Scandinavia	£9,079K	11, 4, 8, 1
*********	Western Germany	£8,210K	8, 11, 4, 1, 10
****	Middle East	£5,557.9K	4, 8, 7, 1
***	Switzerland	£4,905K	11
*****	France	£4,690K	11, 4, 10
**	Africa	£4,462.5K	1, 4, 7
****	Benelux	£2,204.5K	8, 11, 13
*	Near East	£ 700K	7
**	Italy	£ 545K	8
***	Spain	£ 350K	8, 12
*	Japan	£ 88K	8, 11
**	Israel	£ 87.3K	8, 11
*	Singapore	£ 6.3K	8
*	China	£ 5.5K	1
*	Austria	£ 1.8K	1
*	Greece/India/Pakistan		12
*	Hong Kong/Korea		12

For 'Class of Business' refer to classifications in the Questionnaire
(Appendix 1).

Conclusions

Comparisons between the responses to different questions revealed several key features of language use in South West England:

1. Firms are attempting to cope for most of the language applications. But the major area in which they are looking for more expertise than they can supply themselves is in writing trade documents.

2. In FRENCH and GERMAN, the firms are at least twice as reliant on their own staff **except**, significantly, in the crucial factors of oral or documentary presentation of their own products, and in interpreting their competitors'/suppliers' literature. In SPANISH and RUSSIAN they appear to be holding their own; but in ITALIAN the picture is less clear. In ARABIC, help is being enlisted from outside to deal with half of the skills involved, especially in the written mode; while in JAPANESE there is no discernible pattern owing to the size of the response.

3. Educational curricula: our findings reflect the fact that French and German, which are the languages most commonly taught in the UK are the ones most used by firms in this region, but some sector–specific expertise is sometimes required.

4. The comparison of Questions 8 and 4 (see Appendix 1) set alongside that of Question 6 and 8 reveals that the four languages which feature most prominently in the clusters in both comparisons are French, German, Italian and Arabic.

5. There is a healthy lack of complacency in that the firms which have endeavoured to conduct business in their clients' language still perceive that their trade performance could be improved by an extension of their language facilities and expertise.

Chapter 11

FOREIGN LANGUAGES IN DEMAND BY INDUSTRY AND COMMERCE IN THE SUSSEX AREA
Colin Bearne

Introduction

On a number of separate occasions during 1985–6 the Language Centre at Sussex University was approached by industrial, commercial enterprises or government institutions and asked to provide specialist language instruction, either for individuals or groups. These requests often suggested that there might be specific areas in which the Centre might develop such services to Industry. It was therefore decided to conduct a survey of local language needs. The area chosen was that of Brighton, Hove, Horsham and mid–Sussex. One of the main aims of conducting such a survey was to discover which languages are most in demand and for what purposes. On the basis of the results we would be able to determine how the Language Centre at Sussex might best provide for these needs.

The Sample

The Brighton area contains only a few firms which are sufficient in size to be obvious targets. In addition the original mailing list was compiled on the basis of a careful perusal of the Brighton and Horsham Yellow Pages. Firms were selected on the basis of whether at first sight they seemed likely to be involved in import–export of goods, services or people. On this basis, a sample of 354 was arrived at. These included commercial institutions, such as banks and finance houses, educational institutions, training colleges and professional organisations. The last category, and numerically by far the greatest, was manufacturing industry – in particular, electronics and precision engineering – but also timber importers–exporters and dealers in fur, jewels, and so on.

The geographical area covered by the survey was that of a radius of approximately 40 km around Brighton, but it excluded certain small industrial areas on the Kent and Surrey borders.

The Questionnaire

A simple questionnaire was drawn up with the aid of the Pickup Scheme's Sussex University representative Harry Phillips. The Pickup

Scheme also helped bear the cost of mailing the questionnaire, which went out during December 1986. The form itself was so designed that recipients either ticked or gave Yes/No answers, adequate space was also left for those who wished to provide more detailed information.

A pre-stamped envelope was provided. Replies came in several days after the original mailing and continued to arrive into 1987. In the event some 100 replies were received giving a reponse rate of 28%.

The Findings

The questionnaire was prefaced with a brief introduction explaining its aims, origins and objectives. Then the initial question was simply to discover whether or not the firm/institution had any contact with foreign languages. Of the 100 replies received 53 were positive and 47 were negative. One negative reply implied that all the firm's language needs were adequately catered for by agencies. Another claimed to have sufficient language expertise on their own staff. Two other negative replies were of marginal interest. One was headed "We are not an English Language college, but a secretarial college". Another from a local airport dismissed the questions with the assertion that "English is the international language of flying".

The positive replies (some 15% of the original 354) were evenly divided between firms or institutions who had staff capable of dealing with some foreign language work (24) and those who did not (23). What was interesting here was that 17 of the 24 who had language-trained staff asked for additional language instruction, suggesting a need for additional language skills. Nine of the 47 indicated that although they had dealings with people in non-English speaking countries they did not consider that they needed any further courses or training. It had therefore to be assumed that they conducted their business successfully in English.

Firms were then asked to give some assessment of the way in which they used foreign languages in the conduct of their business. They had been provided with five categories: written, verbal, both written and verbal, social and technical. Although there was bound to be a considerable overlap in practice, these seemed to have been fairly satisfactory categories, and firms had the opportunity of marking more than one box. In the event this produced some apparently confusing statistics in the replies. 22 firms reported their use as mainly verbal, 14 as mainly written and there were 29 responses which showed the use as being a mixture of both verbal and written. As far as the kind of language used was concerned, 25 recorded a use of mainly technical register and only 15 recorded a mainly social application. In so far as these responses showed any preponderant tendency, they seemed to indicate that a larger number of firms estimated their use as mainly verbal and technical.

Surprisingly, only 16 of the positive respondents stated that they used an agency for translating/interpreting. Of the 31 who did not use an agency, 25 firms felt they could benefit from courses of further language instruction. Only two firms seemed to be using agencies and to be satisfied that this took care of all their language needs. On the whole it could be said that though agencies played a role in the way firms approached non–English users there were obviously larger areas of language use which the agencies did not satisfy, either because firms felt they could not do so, or because the volume of work did not justify approaching an agency – for the very simple reason of cost.

Firms were asked whether they thought an audio/video foreign language presentation of their product would help in sales. Two firms already had sales material of this kind. An additional 13 said they were definitely interested and a further two would consider such a presentation as a possibility. In addition firms were required to answer a question about the desirability of an A/V presentation of their product in terms of training clients or clients' employees in the use of machinery. A much smaller number was interested here, 9 definites and one possible. This could possibly suggest something about sales methods, and the kinds of products marketed rather than lack of awareness of A/V training materials on the part of the firms in the sample.

The final set of questions in the questionnaire was of significance for the formation of Language Centre policy towards industry in the future. Respondents were presented with a choice of kinds of language training and asked to select those which were most appropriate to their needs. No mention was made of costs so that this was not allowed to become a deciding factor. The replies to these questions told us a great deal about the size of the firms concerned and the way they perceived their trading operations and use of personnel.

By far the most popular method of instruction chosen was self–study using A/V self–instruct materials. 28 of the positive responses favoured this method of acquiring or reinforcing language skills. 19 of these, 40% of the total question–respondents, asked for self–instruct facilities to be made available after or outside normal working hours. The least popular was special purpose tuition for small groups. This was selected in only 4 cases (8.5%). Size of undertaking and its operations may also be a factor here because considerably more respondents, 14 or 28%, selected special purpose training for individuals. Short intensive introductory courses were favoured by 34% of respondents. It was not made clear to those answering the questionnaire that the instruction need not take place at a Language Centre but could be brought to them in the form of a learning package or tutored course. An awareness of this might materially have affected the replies to this question.

Firms were asked to specify which language or languages were involved in their contacts with non–English speaking countries. Their replies in Table 1 make interesting reading in the light of the continuing debate about the appropriateness or otherwise to industry's needs of the languages taught in Britain's schools. The emergence of French and German at the top of the table, if somewhat surprising, may in one way be reassuring as these are the languages at present most frequently encountered in Britain's schools. On the other hand, geographical proximity and the nature of East Sussex trade and manufacture may be local factors which go towards explaining the relative local importance of these two languages. Several other points need to be noted about the table. The spread of languages itself is indicative of the world–wide nature of the trade in question. In this respect Arabic rates surprisingly low, while Japanese and Chinese among other world languages feature encouragingly frequently.

TABLE 1 Companies' Use of Foreign Languages in Trade Contacts

French	33	German	31	Spanish	25	Italian	16
Chinese	9	Japanese	7	Dutch	4	Arabic	4
Russian	4	Portuguese	3	'Indian'	3	Malay	2
Iranian	2	Tagalog	2	Indonesian	2	Hebrew	1
"Scandinavian"	1	Tamil	1	Thai	1	Krio	1

Before proceeding to look at the kind of instruction favoured and relating this to the list of languages, it should be pointed out that in order to maintain a degree of simplicity several language issues were left unclear when it came to analysing the responses. No effort had been made, for example, to separate European French (France, Belgium, Switzerland) from French as spoken in the former French territories abroad, principally in Africa and Asia. This was equally true of Spanish and, to a certain extent, of Portuguese. Bearing this in mind it could be argued that our trade with German speakers in Europe (FRG/GDR, Austria and Switzerland) is running at a higher rate than with any other language group in Europe.

Another and more varied picture is obtained by putting together the languages recorded with the kind of instruction thought to be required. The same relative balance is evident in Table 2 with the notable entry of Italian onto the scene. The list under this heading is less extensive, and in most cases Centres would have little difficulty in identifying potential tutors, though identifying the precise needs of the small groups and then meeting them – that might prove more difficult. Table 2c illustrates the degree to which individuals are prepared to subject themselves, or possibly their colleagues, to the daunting experience of learning exotic languages. The list is very extensive. 2c also illustrates much the same as 2d in terms of scope.

TABLE 2 Training Requirements

a) Short Intensive Introductory Courses

German	11	French	9	Spanish	8	Japanese	4
Arabic	3	Portuguese	3	Dutch	3	Chinese	2
Indonesian	1	Farsi	1	Hindi	1	Malay	1

b) Special Purpose Tuition for Small Groups

French	4	German	4	Italian	4
Spanish	2	Russian	2	Arabic	2
Chinese	1	Japanese	1	Dutch	1

c) Special Purpose Tuition for Individuals

French	13	German	11	Spanish	8	Italian	7
Japanese	5	Arabic	4	Chinese	4	"Scandinavian"	1
Tagalog	3	Tamil	2	Malay	2	Russian	2
Indonesian	2	Dutch	2	Farsi	2	Portuguese	1
Hindi	1	Thai	3	Greek	1		

d) Access to Self–Instruct Facilities

French	10	German	10	Spanish	7	Japanese	5
Italian	5	Dutch	4	Arabic	4	Chinese	3
Tagalog	2	Thai	2	Farsi	2	Tamil	1
Russian	1	Greek	1	Hindi	1	"Scandinavian"	1

Unsolicited Information

Nearly all of this dealt with the conduct of the survey and comments on the form and the questions. The following remarks, however, illustrate a well publicised attitude in British industry and commerce about the use of foreign languages:

"Greeks and Arabs speak English when dealing with us"

"We have to rely on their secretaries speaking English"

"No language instruction needed – they speak English"

It is also worth noting that a major airport facility appears to have staff trained only in French, German and Spanish.

Concluding Remarks On The Findings

1. The high ranking given to French and German, but particularly French, confirms the emerging picture of French's continued dominance in Southern England, though only slightly ahead of German.

    Furthermore, certain specific reasons account for this dominance:

    i) there is a high proportion of trade conducted locally, i.e. from East Sussex, with mainland French speaking countries; France, Belgium, Luxembourg, Switzerland.

    ii) French is used in trading with other countries where it is still a commercial language – French Africa, India, Oceania.

    iii) French is used in trading with non–Francophone countries e.g. Greece because French is the foreign language available most readily amongst the staff of the firm concerned.

2. The role of translation agencies is an interesting one. Though they are active in solving some problems there are other areas of need where they are not called upon. Most agencies offer a swift professional service, at a price. Cost is an important factor for both large and small enterprises and unless Language Centre services can be shown to be competitive and to give the firm a return for its money, they will not be taken up.

3. Only a minority of firms are interested in an A/V presentation of their product. As far as one can tell, there may be two factors at work here. One has already been alluded to, namely the fear of costs, and the second may be that local firms are simply not producing products which are adaptable for audio and video

presentation. On the other hand, a pilot project might well be undertaken in a local firm, perhaps with Pickup backing, to ascertain the feasibility of this.

4. As a general conclusion it does seem that Language Centres should give greater publicity to their self–instructional facilities, and perhaps make arrangements for them to be available on a wider basis, possibly by keeping them open longer in the evenings and on Saturdays.

   There would also seem to be an immediate need to improve self–instruct holdings in Arabic, Chinese, Japanese and African and Asian languages generally. The results in this respect would seem to support the findings of the Parker Committee and hopefully money made available by this committee through the UGC could be used to develop holdings in this area.

5. In German, French and Spanish there is a very obvious need for short intensive courses for groups. Most Language Centres are well enough equipped to mount such courses – which need not necessarily be at introductory or beginners level. In a number of other languages, Japanese, Chinese, Arabic, Italian, Portuguese, Language Centres very often run courses in all or some of the list. Firms may have a vision of these as "exotic" languages and may simply be unaware of what is available. Once again publicity would seem to be at the root of things. It is a matter of bringing together firms with existing courses and then proceeding to structure special courses for the needs of industry.

6. Finally, the survey showed a vast range of languages being used. Special purpose tuition in all these (as opposed to self–instruct facilities) is not something that all Language Centres can readily provide. There is, however, a potential need and one way of solving it, say in the case of Dutch or SE Asian languages, is for Language Centres to keep a register of language informants and act as a regional 'facilitating agency' – identifying needs and supplying tutors, often on a one–to–one basis for interested individuals. Identifying such informants is not an easy matter, but advertisements in a university community which is multi–lingual will normally produce initial contacts.

SUPPLEMENT

In order to reflect some of the employment background to the survey, a monitoring exercise was carried out on advertisements requiring foreign language proficiency which had appeared in the Brighton area press over a three month period.

Altogether 31 posts were advertised:

> 12 commercial and secretarial,
> 9   EFL teaching,
> 10 teachers of foreign languages in schools

16 of these posts were full time and 15 temporary

2) Languages mentioned in the advertisements:

> French   13
> German   10
> English 9
> Spanish 3
> Latin   1

Other jobs simply mentioned "fluency in a second foreign language" – or similar phrases.

3   Jobs in UK : 24
    Outside   : 7

4   Teaching jobs in foreign language by school

    State   7
    Independent   2

5   Language as a main skill or equal 23
    Ancillary   8

A majority of the posts advertised specified 'spoken' ability. Some also specified particular qualifications required in the language.

– PART II –

THE VIEW FROM INDUSTRY AND TRAINING PROVIDERS

Chapter 12

LANGUAGES IN A MULTINATIONAL BUSINESS[1]
Peter Blackburn

"We are part of the community of Europe,
and we must do our duty as such."

One might imagine that these words came from the lips of Heath or Churchill: in fact it was William Gladstone on the 10 April 1888 – a century ago. This example serves to show that progress on matters international is often very slow. We are **still** debating our role and attitude to Europe a century later. I feel sometimes that progress is just as slow with the British and their linguistic attitudes and aptitudes.

First, before I expand on my attitudes as a businessman to foreign languages, I would like to give you a clear picture of my company, Rowntree plc, and its approach to linguistic skills. I hope that this is representative of many other companies who adopt an approach similar to ours. Certainly I know that many of the views I express are shared by many others.

Rowntree plc is the new name for Rowntree Mackintosh which was formed by the merger of Rowntree and Mackintosh in 1969. Rowntree originated in the 18th Century, although the real development was in the late 19th Century and early 20th Century under Joseph and Seebohm Rowntree, the famous social pioneers. The Mackintosh business started in a Halifax pastry cook's shop in the late 19th Century. Now we are involved in food manufacture and marketing around the world, and are best known for our confectionery.

In 1986 the company's turnover was £1,290m with factories and subsidiary companies established in 11 different countries. We now employ 16,300 people in the UK and 16,000 non–UK citizens around the world (including 3,600 in Europe), totalling 32,300 in all. The company is truly international and sells to over 140 markets round the world.

Company Organisation

We are organised with a Group Board. Under the Group Board there are 4 regions, each of which controls several companies. Each subsidiary company has a local board of management reporting to a Regional Chairman who is a Group Board member. Abroad, the Company staff are predominantly local nationals. Of necessity, RM Worldwide is heavily involved in the business of languages and we are firm believers in the importance of learning and applying languages not only as exporters to our markets abroad, but also in the 11 major markets where we actually run foreign businesses. Across the Group we have men and women, multi–functional specialists, who travel to many countries. There is therefore an important need for considerable language ability, both European and non–European, on a daily basis. A survey carried out some time ago amongst our then European HQ staff showed that only 15% had no knowledge of a foreign language.

For our business, foreign languages are therefore most important *not just for the development of the business externally*, but also *internally*. For example, not all our employees speak English – our annual employee report is issued not only in English, we also publish it in five additional languages: Dutch, German, French, Italian and Xhosa.

As far as the relations between business and education go, we believe that it is important that educationalists and the outside world generally should better understand the requirements of the business community. Things can only happen if regular contact is established and maintained between the world of education and business. Following several years of trying to help the education world with data and statistics and case studies on the use of languages in business, we in Rowntree Mackintosh decided to make a video film, which is now widely known, aimed at showing in a visual manner, the practical use of languages at work for the use of educationalists.

What then are our basic perspectives about foreign languages? Some of these I suspect will be 'old hat'; others may be less familiar. However, one must talk about language usage generally and not just at the higher levels; it is important to understand the whole picture which affects the whole academic scale, starting with schools right up to the polytechnics and the universities.

There are eight over-riding points I would like to make, and I know from discussions with other businessmen that these views are pretty representative:-

(1) *English alone is not enough*:

There is a common belief that English is increasingly becoming the international language and that therefore foreign languages are less important to an English speaker, which is expressed in the attitude, "We don't need to bother".

Now it is certainly true that English is increasingly the Number 1 language and that many technical and business terms are American or English.   However, the truth is that as business becomes more international so the need for foreign languages becomes *more*, not *less*, imperative. Business is becoming more international everywhere –
   in Europe, where half of UK trade goes, in the Middle East and in the emerging Far East.   In fact I would go as far as to say that it is a case of 'no language, no business'.

For a start, not all foreign businessmen can speak English and even those that do, do not always want to. If we cannot speak German to the Germans, then the Japanese will.   Secondly, it is a common courtesy to show some knowledge of the local language. Thirdly, in a situation where you are dealing with foreign daughter companies, you need to know what is going on, to maintain control, to assess and develop people, to manage the business, and deal with people at all levels. You have to be able to communicate and thus language skill is essential. If you are serious about business abroad, then you must be serious about foreign language skills.

(2) *A foreign language skill on its own is rarely sufficient in
      business*:

We should bear in mind, however, that language skills are additional or supportive to the other skills required by business, which is fundamentally different to the world of education. Only in an in-company interpreting/translation department is language an end in itself, yet for many other areas additional language skills are often required, for example, in despatch and distribution departments where problems have to be quickly handled across *several different languages*, such as getting a French lorry driver through factory picket lines.

In running a business we primarily need functional experts. So we recruit people who are qualified as accountants/finance men, engineers and production personnel, product personnel (chemists etc), marketing specialists, advertising and market research experts, salesmen and women, secretarial staff and general administrators. Whilst we recruit all these people for their prime skills, any language ability is an important asset and in comparing two people of equal ability for a job, the one with any language ability would be likely to get preference.

(3) *The Business and Commercial relevance of foreign languages must be better understood by both educationalists/teachers and pupils:*

I have been surprised in talking to teachers and educationalists how little is known about industry and the workings of a business. **There must be closer contact.** For this reason the Rowntree Mackintosh video on foreign languages is concerned with stressing the relevance of languages in the real world illustratively. As far as schoolchildren are concerned, I am often disappointed in the attitude of English children to languages compared with their Continental counterparts. English children often see their French or German as just another subject, another GCSE level in an overall target, rather than as a practical, living and useful skill. Only by understanding better about one of the end uses can the relevance of languages be better put across. The problem under the present educational system of splitting Arts and Sciences at 'A' level means languages are very often dropped at 16, if not even earlier. A way to counter this should be found.

The signs that industry and education are getting closer are very encouraging. Industry Year has helped this; the Festival of Languages has forged a lot of links both regionally and nationally, for which much of the funding came from industry and commerce.

(4) *Languages are much more easily and better learnt when young:*

Our experience of later learning is not very successful unless the learner has natural flair. Intensive, or crash courses are not very successful unless they build on some language skills which have been put there earlier. For older learners there are problems of time and family commitments, whilst young people have more time and more opportunity and the young brain is more adaptable. Therefore it is important to realise that the **process must start much earlier** in the educational system. Foreign countries tend to start languages much sooner than in England and with a real–life emphasis. We, for example, receive requests for exchanges at an earlier age from abroad – i.e. as young as 8–10 years old.

British children should be encouraged to be less reticent and more expressive and forthcoming. Compared with Continental children, British children tend to go into their shells and be afraid of 'having a go'. Teachers should put more emphasis on encouragement to greater self– expression. But possibly this is also due to the earlier start made by Continental children.

(5) *Importance of spoken word in business:*

Much of the important business is conducted orally; e.g. on the telephone, across the table, at meetings, or over dinner. For most people ability to communicate in the spoken word is more important than the written word. The experts do the written word. Yet, even those traditionally not associated with languages, not associated with the written word, are beginning to make contact with developing technology, with languages and, in particular, with the spoken word, such as the Company's secretarial staff.

(6) *Importance of Understanding the cultural and educational background of different nationalities (almost as important as language):*

In business, as in other matters, you do not deal with a Frenchman in the same way as a German, and an Italian is a case apart. In the Middle East a burp is a way of expressing gratitude for a good meal!

Historically, the British education system has put too much emphasis on classical literature; e.g. Molière, Goethe, Dante. However, I think that we need much more emphasis on today's world – i.e. on understanding the recent history and culture of each country. It is important to realise that people do business in different ways in each country. For example, business attitudes in Germany are geared to the long term, largely as a result of the German fear of inflation. For instance, the German approach to Balance Sheets and Accounts is fundamentally different to our own, due to the Weimar republic and the massive inflation of the early 20s. Germans are prepared to take a longterm view and their bankers will lend heavily on assets and material things. Also, German management and unions negotiate wages in a fundamentally different way. Their overall approach is one of directness, discipline and a liking for leadership. By contrast, there is in Italy a strong sense of 'bella figura'. This is very important in the way we position our products, such as 'After Eight', in relation to local products.

On the other hand, we must try to understand how foreigners see the English and our qualities. For example, the position of being an 'Island Race' has affected many of our attitudes. Also, 'understatement' is a common national characteristic; we can frequently use 'polite' conversational formulae which carry more direct, but hidden, meanings:

'I'd be grateful if...' = 'You'd better do it or else...'
'Correct me if I'm wrong, but...' = 'Don't you dare contradict me...'

One true example of a peculiar use of English causing a breakdown of communication once came when the English Chairman responded to a Dutch employee's proposal with: "You'd better think about that again!" It came as a complete surprise to the Chairman when the meeting later reconvened and the Dutchman put forward the same proposal again, saying, "I did think about it and I haven't changed my mind."

(7) *Increasing importance of languages other than European:*

In this country there has been an undue over-emphasis on French, whilst we need more thrust on German and other European languages. In business during the past 15 years we have seen a major movement in world markets – with much development of the Middle East and Japan. So Arabic and Japanese are becoming more important, this need not be overstated, but we should be aware of changes in our markets overseas.

My own personal career reflects much of what I have said. After obtaining a language degree I became a Chartered Accountant, then joined Rowntree Mackintosh following a financial career. Some 13 years after graduating I joined the European operation and spent 10 years in General Management there; although I have now transferred to a UK Board function my knowledge of languages can still be most valuable. This is not untypical in business, where language skills can lie dormant and be called upon later to support the other skills that have been acquired along the way.

Summary

i)   We should all encourage a much wider appreciation of the use and importance of languages, *particularly the spoken word;*

ii)   In business, linguistic skills are supportive to other skills;

iii)   Languages are best learnt young; therefore it is important to change attitudes at an early age;

iv)   We need more emphasis on the cultural aspects and recent history of individual countries abroad;

v)   We should be aware of the emergence of new languages in our overseas trade and avoid too much emphasis on French;

vi)   Closer ties between business and the world of education would encourage understanding and higher standards.

In conclusion we believe, as an international company, that languages are very important and make a real contribution to the development of the business.

Reference and Notes

1. This chapter is the edited version of a talk given on a FLAW course organised at Grantley Hall, Ripon, on 26 February 1987.

Chapter 13

MANAGING COMPANY TRAINING PROGRAMMES IN FOREIGN LANGUAGES FOR BUSINESS
Robert Taylor

Initial Considerations In Training Provision

olleges of FE have for many years been providing foreign language training services to industry. However, a major step forward in how this has been organised has taken place in the West Midlands, where two years ago a group of local eductional institutions took the step of establishing a separate agency – IC (Language and Communication Services) Ltd to create a specialist focus for this activity. This has had many advantages both for the institutions involved and for our clients. One of these has been that we have been able to build up a core of experience about what makes successful foreign language training.

Foreign language training is an expensive commodity and any company which has taken the decision to introduce a training programme for its employees will need to consider what kind of approach is most likely to provide value for money for what is, in many cases, a long term commitment. Our experience suggests that successful training requires an approach which is very closely based on meeting the identified training needs of the learners. This needs–based approach succeeds because the learning is directly relevant. The learners are therefore in a position to make use of new language skills at the earliest possible moment. This in turn ensures that the learners' motivation is maintained and learning continues to be successful. By ensuring that a needs–based approach is adhered to and that management of the programme is active we believe that truly cost–effective training is achieved: learners do not waste time on irrelevancies and the pace of learning is maintained.

More and more companies are recognising the advantages which this can bring to the company:

- better communication with overseas customers/contracts resulting in better understanding of overseas business

- enhanced image overseas

- better interpersonal relationships between British and foreign colleagues

- a competitive edge in negotiations overseas

Finally, the spin-off in terms of working relationships between members of the same language learning group can be considerable, resulting in improved in-company communication.

Implementing A Successful Programme

An increasing number of training managers are finding themselves in the position of setting up a language training programme for the first time. This inexperience, coupled with the problems inherent in managing language training programmes, has in the past led to the collapse of the programme – an expensive outcome both financially and in terms of training achievement. The process of implementing a foreign language training programme can be broken down into the four steps, with account being taken of a variety of factors at each step:

1. Select and Group Trainees

Who needs training?
What skills are required?

3. Choose a provider

Flexibility
Facilities
Quality of teaching
Relevance of materials

2. Decide on training mode(s)

Intensive
Drip-feed
Group
One-to-one
Open learning
In plant
School

4. Manage the programme

Recruitment
Start-up
Monitoring
Evaluation

Whilst the distinction between these four steps is to some extent artificial, it is worth considering them separately and in turn.

1. Selecting And Grouping Trainees

The decision to introduce foreign language training into the company will clearly be led by the need for foreign language competence amongst the employees. This need can become apparent to the training manager in a variety of ways:

–   a direct approach by an employee or employees

–   existing *ad hoc* training initiatives within the company

–   business developments which will generate a likely training requirement eg a major contract with a Japanese company or the acquisition of a German subsidiary

–   existing overseas business involving employees who have not approached the training manager but who may benefit from training

–   re-organisation, bringing employees into contact with people from overseas where they have not had this contact before.

Once a general need has become apparent the training manager is faced with establishing two key facts, which need to be considered separately: *who* needs training and *what* training do they require.

In a small company the picture may be very clear. In a larger company the picture can be quite complex and the training manager will probably need to conduct a training audit in order to establish a firm base on which to build the training programme. A well conducted audit will:

–   identify who could benefit from training

–   identify which language(s) are required

–   identify which skills are required by which individuals.

An audit can also:

–   identify existing language skills in the company

–   identify valuable sources of cultural/protocol information about particular countries.

It might be possible for the training department to conduct the audit itself, although it will probably be preferable to ask an outside organisation experienced in undertaking this kind of audit (such as IC Ltd) to carry out the work, as an understanding of foreign language teaching is important, especially at the analysis stage.

Having identified who needs the training and what skills are required, the trainees can then be grouped accordingly. It is in making the decision about grouping that mistakes are most often made which lead to problems in the programme later on. Account needs to be taken of a number of factors:

(a) **starting level**
A skilled teacher will cope with a multi-level group, but success will depend on:

> the more advanced being willing and able to help the others. Provided personality and hierarchical considerations rule this out.

> the disparity in the group not being too great. It is not a good idea, for example, to put someone with an 'A' level in with a group of beginners.

(b) **skills required**
Giving ample consideration to the skills that each learner should acquire as a priority is perhaps the single most important consideration in setting up business language learning, and is the key to cost-effectiveness.

One major division in skills might be, for example, the skills required by those who travel to the country and those who don't. Mixing the two inevitably leads to members of the group feeling that they are wasting their time in some lessons. Then there are job-related skills. A group comprising an auditor, a switchboard operator, a secretary, an engineer and two export salesmen would clearly be impossible to teach successfully, since they would all require very different skills.

(c) **hierarchical position**
In some companies the hierarchy is not a factor which needs to be taken into account. Other company cultures are extremely hierarchical and it is important to ensure that this is reflected in the grouping process.

(d) urgency of need

It is pointless to put someone needing the language urgently into a group whose programme is paced over 12 months.

In summary, getting the groups right is vital to the success of the training programme. The inclusion of one individual in a group who 'doesn't fit' can disrupt the group completely. However, economic considerations also have to be taken into account and some compromise will almost certainly be required.

2. Deciding The Training Modes

There are a wide variety of training modes available and the circumstances of personnel will dictate which are most suitable.

(a) Intensive short courses (30–50 hours per week)

Good for: i) getting a beginner off the ground,

ii) brushing up before an important trip,

iii) training rapidly in limited, clearly defined target skills.

Advantages: Gets the learner away from the distractions of the office. Motivation easily managed over a short period.

Disadvantages: Learner under intense pressure – stress is not conducive to language learning.
A 1–3 day settling period is common in which the learner adjusts him or herself to language learning; thus not very cost-effective.
Too much information in too short a space of time – especially if the course offers in excess of 30 hours per week. The amount that a person can absorb in one day is limited. The super-intensive course may be less cost-effective than it appears.
The learner is away from the office. Once away from the school the learner loses all support and impetus; i.e. motivation failure.

(b)   Intensive short course abroad

As above but,
- i)   exposure to the country
- ii)   likely to be motivating
- iii)   more expensive.

(c)   'Drip-feed' courses (2–6 hours per week)

Good for: Maintaining and building skills.

Advantages: Learner only away from the office for a short period each week (especially if training delivered in-plant). Flexible. Learning well-paced.

Disadvantages: Careful thought needs to be given to management of the programme and motivation of the learners. This mode cannot take account of short term deadlines – not really suitable, for example, for pre-visit 'brush up.'

(d)   One-to-one

Good for: All situations.

Advantages: Full account can be taken of the learner's needs, existing abilities and target skills; hence learning is very efficient. Very flexible – learning can be on an appointment basis. Motivation easier to control.

Disadvantages: Lack of contact with other learners. Cost (although speed of learning makes this mode more cost-effective than might at first be apparent).

(e)   Groups

Good for: All situations.

Advantages: Plenty of scope for interaction with other learners.

Disadvantages: Ideally members of a group should have the same achievement level and learning objectives. This can be difficult to arrange. Learning is slower than one to one. Groups are inflexible. If a learner cannot make a session he will fall behind and become de-motivated. (This is especially true of beginners.) If differentindividuals fail to make the session on different occasions over a period of weeks the group is likely to break down.

(f) Open learning

Good for: Supplementary practice to tutored sessions.

Advantages: Very flexible. Privacy to make mistakes. Well used open learning materials will enable the learners to make better use of the tutors time eg by practising skills such as pronunciation away from the classroom. Classroom time can be devoted to skills which need tutor support.
High tech equipment can give a boost to motivation.

Disadvantages: Tapes used in isolation can give the learner intellectual understanding of the language but in order to develop the confidence to use the language effectively contact with other speakers is needed. Motivation outside a tutored structure is difficult to maintain. Open learning material currently available is often inadequate for one or more of the following reasons:

–   it lacks business orientation

–   it is poorly structured for working alone

–   the methodology is out-dated and ineffective

3.   Choosing The Provider

Having identified the training needs and given consideration (probably in consultation with the group of learners) to the most suitable delivery mode, the training manager is in a much stronger position to select a training provider able to offer the appropriate facilities and flexibility. However, it should not be forgotten that the cost-effectiveness of the programme will depend on the quality of what happens in the classroom and that the most important factor in the success of the programme is likely to be the teacher. It is a common misconception that any speaker of a foreign language can teach it, and in particular that a native speaker will make a better teacher than someone who has learned the foreign language.

At lower levels of attainment an English speaker may be preferred as he/she will possibly have more insight into the problems of the English learner. At higher levels a native speaker may be able to offer a greater variety of expression and a more authentic accent.

However, the primary concern should be that the teaching is provided by someone who is skilled in teaching a foreign language to adults. The general skills which should be looked for are:

- an ability in the teacher to clearly understand the requirements of the learners and to produce lessons to help meet those requirements, ie an approach which uses needs as its base rather than the progression of a particular textbook or the structure of the language.

- an ability to produce stimulating lessons in which the emphasis is on the learners to speak, listen etc, rather than on the teacher explaining things.

- an ability to deliver the lesson in the foreign language from the beginning.

The support which the teacher receives from the training organisation is also important, especially if the training is to include specialist technical elements.

4.   Managing The Programme

The management of language training is really about the management of the motivation of the learners. Since motivation really is the key to language learning success it is worth putting some effort and thought into how this can be managed at all stages.

During **recruitment:**

- the advantages of possession of the language skills should be emphasised

- it should be made clear that the training is based on **achievable** and **relevant** skills

- the backing of training personnel and management should be made clear.

At the **start–up** of the programme:

- it is a good idea to have an informal session with wine and food of the country concerned. Fostering interest in the country is an important aspect of long–term motivation and such a session can be combined with discussion of the programme content.

- it may be appropriate to take a small deposit off the learners, refundable only if the course is completed.

In the course of the programme *monitoring* is essential. The process of conducting the needs audit and grouping the trainees will inevitably have led to broad objectives being established. In consultation with the provider these can be developed into a full programme for each group or individual. Where economic constraints dictate that learners with different needs appear in the same group, *it is essential that the content of the programme should be negotiated with the group*. Indeed, it is essential that any programme is agreed by the teacher, the learners and the training manager. That way everyone is clear about the direction and objectives of the programme from the beginning. That direction and those objectives also provide the basis for the monitoring of the programme. We believe that monitoring should be jointly conducted by the company training manager and the training organisation.

Initial monitoring should take place early in the programme in order to sort out any teething troubles, and then at negotiated intervals after that. The objective of any monitoring should be to assess how well the objectives are being achieved and to negotiate a solution to any problem that has arisen. This might be, for example, to introduce a new element into the programme and delete something else. It might be to adjust the programme in the light of the fact that the learners are not able to complete as much work away from the classroom as they had anticipated. The important thing is that the training manager should remain in touch with what is happening and be aware as soon as anything changes which is likely to prejudice the fully successful outcome of the training.

At the end of the programme the company may wish to arrange some kind of **validation**. This validation might be external where the examination concerned is relevant to the programme, or in the case of a more specialised programme the provider should organise this for the company. Consideration might also be given to an award of some kind for the most successful learners. This cost need not be high, but the help to motivation can be considerable. In addition there can be valuable spin–offs in terms of both internal and external publicity.

CONCLUSIONS

In summary, a well managed foreign language training programme can bring many advantages to a company. All too often, however, foreign language training is not as well managed as it could be, thus creating demoralisation on the part of the learners and disillusion on the part of training management. Careful thought and planning of the management of the programme will ensure its maximum cost–effectiveness and benefit.

Chapter 14

LANGUAGE TRAINING AT ICI'S WILTON SITE FOR CHEMICALS & POLYMERS LTD
Doug Embleton

Introduction to ICI and Foreign Languages

The Wilton complex (near Middlesborough, Cleveland), is one of the largest of its type in the world and is the major site of the petrochemicals and plastics sector of Chemicals and Polymers. About 15,000 people are employed in petrochemicals and plastics operations in Western Europe of whom some 12,000 work in the UK.

In terms of world-wide sales this represents ICI's largest sector and with production sites in the UK, France, Belgium, Holland, Germany and Switzerland – it is truly an international business. The skills of the people whom it employs range from process and production techniques through engineering, sales, marketing, planning, finance, and computing to the research-oriented disciplines of chemistry, physics, mathematics and metallurgy. A whole range of language barriers are crossed daily, involving customers, suppliers and colleagues in different countries.

A language training package has been developed, at Wilton, over the last 15 years to meet these needs and it is the object of this paper, firstly, to outline the philosophy and stucture of the language training packages at Wilton; and, secondly, to publish the results of a language training survey carried out on-site in 1987.

Language Training at Wilton

The Languages Unit is a small operation in terms of the number of in-house linguists which it employs – 4 in all. The broad role of the Unit is to support the business of the Group and to ensure that the Group overcomes language barriers as effectively as possible in line with the Group's declared aims of promoting internationalism and fostering our view of Western Europe as our home market.

The Languages Unit at Wilton provides the following basic services:
–   written and oral translations, interpreting, assistance with the

production of sales and product literature in foreign languages, language training and an on–going procedure for self–evaluation – the 'Language Audit'

The first Language Audit was carried out in the early Seventies and although the Languages Unit was at that time providing a professional translating, interpreting and publicity literature service, a vital ingredient was seen to be missing – 'language awareness'. There was a great need for more of our staff to be aware of the importance of languages so that the many key areas of our activities which involved foreign languages could be handled more efficiently.

The requirement which emerged from the first Language Audit was of the need to enable staff to 'help themselves' by acquiring and using foreign language skills. It was clear that in such a large organisation with an increasingly European outlook many people and thus the business itself would be assisted by an ability to add secondary language skills to primary job skills. Secondly, the Languages Unit had to become less of an ivory tower or backroom service and integrate itself fully with some of the broader language requirements of the organisation.

The Philosophy

The language training packages which were initiated as a result of the Audit were based and are still based on one of the following criteria for attendance at in–house classes: the acquisition of language skills must be (a) of immediate benefit; (b) of benefit in the foreseeable future; or (c) of potential benfit.

In (b) and (c) we are 'training for stock' in addition to meeting current needs; indeed, our experience has consistently confirmed the advantages of a longer acquisition period of weekly classes over the short, sharp shock of a Crash Course.

The training is not aimed at producing staff who can handle problems requiring the professional language skills. In fact, it usually emphasises the difficulties and pitfalls involved in specialised language work. We are therefore not aiming at total fluency amongst a majority of staff. In its simplest terms 'language awareness' entails the perception on the part of staff that our foreign customers and colleagues not only speak languages other than English, but also have a tendency, for cultural reasons, to think in different ways and to have distinct preferences and priorities in the way in which they do business. Language training is not viewed merely as the acquisition of skills on a fluency scale of 0 – 100%, it has to be geared equally to the level of cultural understanding since even 100% fluency is defective without it. It is aimed at seeing the other person's point of view and understanding why he has his own perception and perspectives. The training must also, of course, ensure that our staff feel comfortable and professional in their transactions with foreign customers. Time and time again, feedback has confirmed that even a modest knowledge of a language has not only created the right impression but has created an 'equilibrium of power' in transactions.

Above all, the support which the management gives to language training has now been consistent and prolonged over a number of years. Lingering illusions that there are quick or painless ways of achieving language proficiency have been dispelled, despite the general tendency in industry and commerce for language training to be viewed as an 'on demand' type of requirement rather than a longer term plan. However, the need for language training in industry is still imposed by certain circumstances which leave very little time for effective progress to be made. This can apply to both the individual ("I have been seconded to a job in Germany starting in 2 months' time and I can only devote 10 days to a course") and to the organisation ("We have signed a contract for sales to Japan. It might be an idea to do some language training – as long as it doesn't take up too much time"). It is our experience that an in-house language training system needs to be permanent, flexible, identifiable and easily accessible.

The Structure

Resources and administration

One of the Language Unit's offices, the 'Language Training Room', not only houses many of the training materials, but is also used for tuition involving small groups. Larger groups are taught in the various conference rooms at the Wilton Centre, but the Language Training Room is the identifiable clearing house for all language training activities. Any matters of broad policy or development are handled by the Senior Linguist. The general administration of the in-house classes is carried out by a part-time Language Training Officer who is also one of the teachers. All the teachers, who include several nationals, are employed on a part-time consultancy basis. Materials which are used include recorded courses, portable cassette players, video tapes and foreign journals. The Languages Unit operates a lending library of recorded language courses which are available to all members of staff.

In-house classes

Weekly 2-hour in-house classes are provided at various levels in German and French; e.g. in 1986–87 a total of 12 classes were running and students are prepared for the LCCI Examinations held every Summer at the Wilton Centre.

The classes are the cornerstone of the language training system at Wilton. One of the most difficult things to predict in industry and commerce is whether an individual will at some time in his or her career require knowledge of a foreign language. The long-term acquisition period provided by the classes ensures that at least some of the people who eventually find they **will** require a foreign language have already become accustomed to the 'language learning habit'. For other people, the need for and use of a foreign language at work is only intermittent and regular classes are the ideal vehicle for bringing their languages up to standard.

In-house individual tuition

In-house individual tuition is provided, usually in 2-hour sessions, to cater for a variety of situations. For example, the very people who should be attending the classes are sometimes unable to do so because of (foreign) travel commitments. Individual tuition on a flexible timetable basis enables them to derive maximum benefit from the facilities available at Wilton. This type of tuition is also provided to students who are about to be seconded abroad by the Company. The individual tuition is used as a starter before an external crash course and as a bridge in between the weeks spent away on the external crash course. Such impending secondments usually involve the whole family and arrangements are often made to provide individual tuition to members of the secondee's family, again on a flexible basis.

In-house group tuition

Certain key projects or Departments provide ideal conditions for setting up classes specifically aimed at covering their individual language requirements.

Recent examples have been:

- a group class in Brazilian Portuguese for a team involved in constructing and commissioning a new plant in Brazil.

- tuition in Italian for a small team involved in market research.

- a German class arranged specifically for the after-sales service people of one particular product.

External Courses

The Languages Unit provides a bridge between the language training facilities available at Wilton and those available on external courses. Many members of staff are sent on such courses but they have a continuous 'life support line' from Wilton.

Some of the external course requirements are highly specialised (for example, Japanese, or Korean) and for these we would seek courses which provided a considerable degree of cultural, as well as linguistic, input. In general, when advice is given to staff who are about to embark on a crash course we attempt to retain their optimism within the boundaries of feasibility and reality since we view language acquisition and its subsequent **successful** use as a long-term process and as a process which only really succeeds if the student has a consistently good experience. Thus, we clearly aim to use external language courses which also recognise these factors.

Wilton Language Training Survey, 1987

During February 1987 a survey was conducted amongst staff at the Wilton site of Chemicals and Polymers Ltd. who were receiving language training.

The main aims of the survey were:

(a) to determine the range and relative importance of language skills used;

(b) to confirm existing feedback from individuals that language skills were becoming *increasingly* important and could significantly influence the attitudes of foreign customers and colleagues;

(c) to confirm one of the main criteria of our in-house language training package, the concept of 'training for stock'. Many people who initially attend the classes have a *potential* need for language skills in their jobs. This potential need frequently materialises and the individual has then the advantage of a longer term, measured experience of language study;

(d) to analyse the relevance of language studies at school to present needs;

(e) to gather real-life experiences and comments.

A questionnaire was sent to 117 people who were either attending in-house classes (the majority) or receiving individual tuition. The response rate was 68%. Several parameters should be mentioned before discussing the results:

–   ICI is probably atypical of most British firms in that, as a British parent multinational, it has major selling companies in many countries and its Company language is English. Thus, many of its UK employees who visit foreign customers are accompanied by local staff who effectively act as go-betweens or interpreters.

–   The increased need for language skills which was revealed by the survey *in spite of* this linguistic cushion of local support could well indicate an even greater need in other exporting organisations.

–   Many of the people who replied are highly self-motivated individuals.

–   The survey was carried out at the Wilton Site (Middlesbrough, Cleveland), but is not necessarily representative of other ICI sites.

The major questions posed by the questionnaire and the responses to these were as follows:

Did you study any foreign language(s) at school?

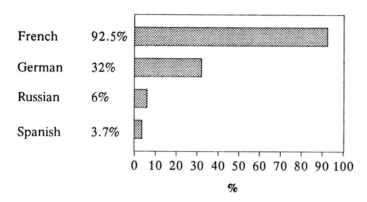

The predominance of French was anticipated. The extremely low figure for Spanish was alarming in the light of the amount of business conducted with Spanish–speaking countries.

Do you feel that the language knowledge with which you were equipped at school was (a) adequate for (b) relevant to current needs?

(a)			(b)	
NO	66%		NO	85%
YES	34%		YES	15%

The overriding comment from the 85% who felt that the language studies at school had not been relevant was that they had not been encouraged to use a foreign language communicatively. There was also a strong feeling that very little had been learned about the culture of the countries concerned. Some of the comments received were:

"Language at school was treated as translation, not as a communicative method."

"I still feel that I can read French but have difficulty in holding a conversation."

"We were taught how to pass an exam, not how to converse in the language."

Do you think that a grammar–based approach to language training is important?

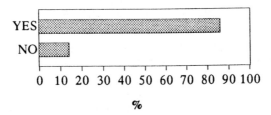

The majority who favoured a 'grammar approach' stressed that it must be closely linked with the acquisition of communicative skills.

"Yes – it gives a strong framework for future development."

"Definitely yes, if ultimately a high standard is to be achieved."

"I like to understand the grammar in order to feel confident about saying anything."

Reasons for current language study

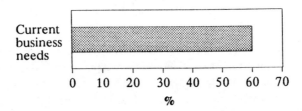

All of the following comments and figures are based on these 60% of respondents.

Language skills used/required in job

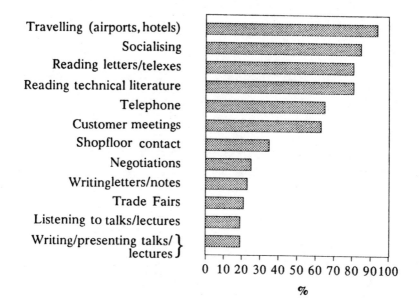

Provide specific examples of when your knowledge of a language in any of the above activities proved especially useful

The importance of socialising as an 'ice breaker' was mentioned in many of the replies:

"Talking socially has led to greater insight and a better relationship."

"Entertaining customers in the DDR is really handicapped by not being able to order in German."

Some of the other comments were:

"I travel to factory 'X' where in general the lower management does not speak English."

"Shopfloor contact has proved very useful in gaining cooperation during product trials."

"I gave a lecture in German, reporting results of a technical project to scientists at company 'X' – a terrifying experience!"

Has your knowledge of a foreign language influenced the attitude of foreign customers or colleagues towards you?

YES: 90%

Perhaps the most pertinent comments were:

"My abilities in spoken Japanese, limited as they initially were, produced two main reactions from my Japanese customers. Firstly, an amazed silence. Secondly – respect."

"I find that more information can be obtained from people if they can talk freely in their own language rather than having to concentrate on speaking mine."

"Yes. ICI is regarded in the German–speaking market as a 'foreigner'. It is vitally important that when called in to discuss or solve a technical problem we can give as good if not better service than our German competitors. This includes speaking their language."

And finally:

Have foreign languages become increasingly important in your job?

YES: 73%

"Yes, it's expected."

"My job could not be done effectively without German."

"Absolutely vital for the future."

Conclusion

Let there be no mistake, in an increasingly competitive world market the likelihood of more people in industry requiring language skills is increasing. We believe that the ready availability of in–house language training facilities and expertise at Wilton and in other parts of ICI is an expression of our long–term commitment to respond to these requirements.

Acknowledgements

The author gratefully acknowledges the assistance with the survey which was provided by Mrs Edie Robinson, Language Training Officer at Wilton.

Chapter 15

LANGUAGE TRAINING AT PEUGEOT TALBOT
Marion Smart

The Company's Need For French In The UK

The Peugeot SA Group employs about 170,000 people throughout Europe. In the UK Peugeot Talbot operations are based at 6 sites in and around Coventry where more than 4,000 people are employed. The UK operations are very closely linked with the parent company. Production and facilities engineers have to adapt French methods and procedures to those used in the UK and quality engineers work in close co-operation with their counterparts in France. French computer systems have been linked in to computer systems in the UK. Body shells and panels, which are made in France, must be held in readiness for the assembly line. Stocks of other parts, some of which come from France, have to be monitored and replenished on a day-to-day basis. A working knowledge of French is therefore vital in many departments.

History Of Language Training

Peugeot Talbot has evolved an on-going language training programme, now running for over 15 years, with approximately 120 students at any given time. All but 6 are studying French. There is, in addition, a small requirement for Spanish and English for French personnel. Originally an in-house programme for self-tuition was set up with a number of individual mini language labs dispersed throughout the Company, plus the availability of postal tuition. Soon it was discovered that a live tutorial system was needed and tutors were provided by the local technical college, using the BBC Radio/TV course, so to give the students contact with everyday French from real life.

As our involvement with Peugeot grew, intensive or accelerated tuition was provided by an outside agency. Eventually, and mainly for financial reasons, an entirely in-house programme was set up with all tuition both intensive and regular provided by one agency, CMD Language Services, which remains the present situation at Peugeot Talbot.

Analysis Of Needs

The need to learn French arises on two levels within the Company: for certain key people French is a tool vital to their job and tuition is scheduled according to the time available. Where possible, forward planning allows for up to a year of semi–intensive tuition in readiness for a new post. In other cases, tuition goes on concurrently with the students work schedule.

For many other people, however, knowledge of French is a useful addition to their work skills, giving them ready ability to cope with documents and telephone calls, rather than using a colleague as a translator or interpreter. In both types of situation the need is assessed by line managers in conjunction with the personnel manager and functional director. Managers appreciate the long term commitment which is required to master a language and have to consider carefully all the factors before signing permission for a person to study French in works time. On the other hand, about 30 people are seeking to overcome this problem by requesting after–hours classes, a need we expect to fill in the near future.

The Present Language Course

The aims of the present course fall into two distinct categories;

(a) to teach listening and speaking skills, and the reading ability which comes along with these;

(b) to convey aspects of French life and culture which will help students to understand and relate to their French counterparts.

In terms of syllabus and materials, we follow a general language course, with the emphasis on aural/oral communicative skills, which moves through the range of ability levels, from complete beginners to advanced. We avoid using a specifically business–oriented course since our students come from various departments, each using a different specialist register of technical or business French. We have found that they are quickly able to acquire the necessary technical vocabulary from the documents which come into their offices every day.

Course tutors also devise additional material, which supplements the basic course, in order to provide practice on specific points of structure, grammar or usage. In addition, we use magazine and newspaper articles, our parent Company's own publications, and any topical material, including suitable snippets of video news which will encourage group participation in a lively discussion.

We are presently looking for an up-to-date course, preferably using only the target language which progresses thoroughly and steadily through the complexities of learning and practising a language. It must have accompanying audio material for groups and individual use with cassettes priced realistically so that each student can have his own practice material.

Provision Of Tutors

The 11 part-time tutors who are supplied on a sessional basis by the outside agency maintain close co-operation with the Training Department on course materials, methods of teaching and the organisational details of the language training programme.

French native speakers are used for intermediate and advanced level students. For beginners, English tutors with a good command of spoken French are preferred as we find they have a clearer appreciation of the difficulties which a beginner encounters. The French native speaker has usually been taught more formal grammar than his/her English opposite number and consequently finds it difficult to adjust to the lack of a structural base awareness at this level.

Duration

Our experience of the past 7 years, also confirmed by figures released by the Training Department of our parent company in 1980, indicate that a complete beginner will require on average 500/600 hours of tuition, plus several hours of home study per week, in order to reach a level which enables them to give presentations in French and to join in the cut-and-thrust of decision-making meetings (see the Language Competence Chart in Appendix B). Previous knowledge obviously gives a base and a pool of vocabulary to draw on which facilitates mastery of the language. Many mature students starting from scratch seem only able at best to acquire a somewhat thin veneer of the language even after prolonged study, whilst an 'O' and 'A' level pass usually reduces this time by 150 or 300 hours respectively.

From our experience those who have tackled one European Language previously have a head start when faced with having to learn a second or subsequent language – strong reasons, therefore, for learning a language at school. We have also found that a student's results are best where studies are combined with regular visits to France. A student with a wife or children who share his interest and study along with him has an additional advantage. Holidays in France, friendships with French families, a love for the country, all these are factors which add incentives to serious study of the language and confirm the importance of integrative motivation.

For most students, a weekly period of 2 1/2 hours is arranged, so that in practice, they may well be on the programme for 5 or 6 years. For some people, it is sufficient for their work purposes to study to intermediate level and stop after 300/400 hours. We find that even those who drop out early in the programme, find that the little they have learnt is useful in their day–to–day work and helps them, at least, to decipher telexes or answer the telephone.

Organisation And Methods

(1) The 40 classes are arranged at our various sites, with due consideration to the student's level and the provision of a suitable class. The convenience of the venue and its timing are important but have to be secondary considerations, since our programme, which involves moving both teachers and students from site to site, gives us some logistical problems.

(2) Most students work in small groups of between 3 and 6 people. About 15 people, with special needs or demands on their time, are taught on a one–to–one basis. Intensive tuition is arranged for individuals with special work requirements.

(3) Classes are conducted in the target language, with the minimum of formal grammar. The tutor's voice is supplemented by audio cassettes which are also used for personal listening practice. Translation is discouraged so as to avoid the slowing down of the process of communication.

(4) Private study is expected of all students, some of whom give the minimum of an hour or so per week. Others devote several hours a week and a few make the learning of French their hobby. Students are encouraged to take their learning outside the classroom by listening to the radio and cassettes at home or in their car, and by watching the French news, films and TV.

Assessing The Student's Progress

Testing is an important aspect of our language training effort. We use two principal methods:–

i.   By our own internal tests.

ii.   By the LCCI examinations which offer 4 levels of assessment of listening and speaking ability, plus some reading comprehension at the later stages.

We find the LCCI exams suited to our needs and rely on them to be forward–looking and to continue to produce the type and level of test most appropriate to the rapidly changing world of business. Their new Threshold Examination has usefully filled a gap, though perhaps the ability to read telexes as well as letters should be tested, since telex is growing in popularity and possibly overtaking the telephone as a fast and reliable means of communication for doing business.

Present Developments

We are presently developing four finite French courses for four categories of learner within the Company:

(a) Telephone operators and secretaries;

(b) Engineers who need to translate engineering manuals, drawings etc.;

(c) Certain people who have to communicate in French. (Company Policy is for documents to be in the native tongue of the writer);

(d) Employees who want to learn "holiday" French, following the evening class pattern.

Each category has a special need which would be catered for on a tailor-made course lasting 20–50 hours. The full results have yet to be evaluated, however, before the courses become a permanent feature of the programme.

Social Events

We hold French evenings, to enable people to practise their French and to savour French food and atmosphere.

Summary

Enough time has now elapsed for us to look back and see how well our employees have coped with the impact of becoming a French company. We now have a number of competent linguists; there are 50–60 fluent French speakers in the plant and several hundred with enough French to cope with the daily demands created by our liaison with France. Others may never become fluent linguists, but are able to go to meetings and not feel they are in a totally alien world.

The Company's commitment to long-term language training has to be given some credit for the positive attitude to France and French people, which has been remarked upon by visitors from outside. Results are not quantifiable, but this commitment must have contributed to our good relations with our parent company and to the integration of our UK Company into the Peugeot group.

APPENDIX A

SPECIFIC CASES OF NEED FOR FRENCH IN THE WORK PLACE

We have chosen 4 typical jobs as examples of how working for a French Company in the UK affects day-to-day work:

Example 1: Secretary to a Purchasing Director: The Secretary has daily telephone calls to and from France, and contacts French people in order to arrange, cancel or re-schedule meetings. For example, she arranges hotels, planes and has even contacted the pilot of a charter aircraft to re-arrange flight schedules.

Emergencies can also arise in the course of her boss's absence; last minute contacts via non-French speaking colleagues, sometimes at second or third remove, are needed to re-arrange the following day's schedule.

She has telex to decipher or telex operators to contact when there are queries to sort out. There are suppliers to speak to, in order to keep vital parts flowing. She has to read documents, translate or do a precis when necessary.

This secretary has to unravel many problems which her boss would simply not have time to do for himself. French is vital to her work.

Example 2: We also have a secretary with a less strong need for French, who needs to be able to locate people in France for her director, to answer the telephone in brief telephone jargon before she passes the caller on to her chief. She needs to know numbers, have some phrases in reasonable French at the tip of her tongue, and generally provide a courteous front-line for her director.

Example 3: The process engineer is involved with the building of car bodies and in particular with the welding problems which cannot be dealt with on the production line. This means discussing practical details about day–to–day and forward planning. Since the controlling body is our French parent company, whose engineering standards and practices we are following, many practicalities have to be worked through, by referring to drawings in French and holding discussions with French counterparts. The French companies who supply fixtures have to be contacted and our requirements explained in detail to them – usually by telephone and very often in French.

Example 4: A Pre–Production Analyst is involved in the planning at the very first stage of the production of a car. His area is linked into the Peugeot computer system which holds the totality of information about the cars being manufactured currently and in the future.

Records have to be adjusted in line with French engineering requirements, according to modifications which are made to the car in the UK and in France as the process of manufacture evolves.

This analyst has to read the VDU screen, to feed in information, to make frequent telephone contact with non–English speaking colleagues, to read telexes and other technical documents. Occasionally, he may need to attend meetings or take a course of instruction – all this in French.

APPENDIX B

LANGUAGE COMPETENCE CHART

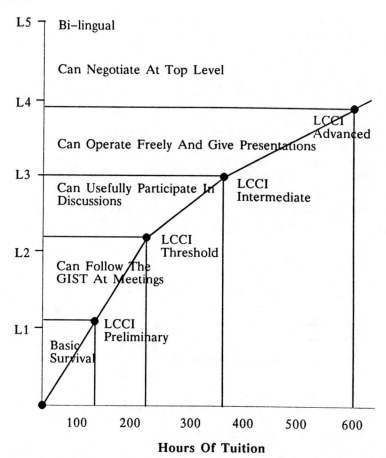

(1) This chart is a guide to the number of hours of tuition required by an average student of a European language.

(2) LCCI = London Chamber of Commerce and Industry (Examinations Board Commercial Education Scheme).

(Article submitted October 1987)

Chapter 16

SUPPLYING THE LANGUAGE TRAINING NEEDS OF MAJOR COMPANIES IN NORTH–WEST ENGLAND
Anne Clarke

The purpose of this paper is, firstly, to analyse the language training requirements of several companies in North–West England, whose language tuition is supplied by the Halton College Languages Unit, identifying any changes in emphasis; secondly, to describe the nature of language tuition and languages packages provided; and, finally, to attempt to define and describe successes of the learners and the benefits to their company.

The companies concerned are almost exclusively in the manufacturing industries, including the chemical industry, glass manufacturing industry, brewing, motor vehicle manufacture, telecommunications, machine tool industry and a manufacturer of spray nozzles. Few representatives of other types of industry have requested or received specifically company–based language tuition, though as individuals they do receive language tuition in other groups .

Tuition has been supplied to the companies in the form of:

- **on–site tuition on a regular weekly basis ('open door' and 'special purpose group');**
- **intensive language tuition;**
- **a flexible 'Business Appointments' package of tuition hours;**
- **"semi–intensive" language training.**

In terms of **student learning hours**, tuition on a regular weekly basis has risen from a total of slightly over 10,000 hours in 1983 to 16,000 in 1987, surpassing by far the combined number of student learning hours in all the other three categories, which, apart from 'Business Appointments', have not exceeded 100 student hours in any of the past five years. This decline in intensive modes of tuition would seem to indicate that companies may be relying less on *ad hoc* measures to meet their needs. They recognise that intensive courses are a less effective manner of achieving and maintaining language skills and certainly the least cost-effective.

The indication that the companies are increasingly adopting a definite and longer-term policy on language training is clearly apparent from the demand for on-going weekly special-purpose group packages. In the past three years an average of just below 5,000 student learning hours per annum has been commissioned mainly for German, Spanish and Italian. German tuition has led the field in all four modes of language training supplied by Halton College. The fact German is the *lingua franca* of Eastern Europe has particularly enhanced its commercial value. It has a 2,000 hour lead over French, followed by Spanish with a slightly narrower differential. Japanese, on a smaller scale, was in fourth position, until recently, when Italian overtook it.

Language Skills and Company Objectives

Many companies are seeking to expand their foreign markets and increase their export sales, and regard language skills as essential in meeting this objective. In a recent survey of our language course participants, much comment was made of the fact that the chief business competitors to the UK are invariably more proficient in languages than are our business people. This is most keenly felt during meetings and negotiations when the British are automatically at a disadvantage. The Germans sell to the French in French, to the English in English etc. – a decided advantage for the Germans, as their overseas sales figures demonstrate.

One member of the Export Department of a large company, with responsibility for South America, pointed out:

"It always flatters the customer if an attempt is made to speak his language. I believe it was a Japanese businessman who said that he used to think that the language of commerce was English. He now realises that it is, in fact, the native language of the customer."

A Technical Product Manager with responsibility for representing his company's interests in the USA, Canada, West Germany, Australia and Japan sought to attain basic skills in German and Japanese. His reasons for learning Japanese are representative of many language learners:

- to gain an insight into the language;
- to understand the customers of the country;
- to show commitment to the company's overseas distributors:
- as an ice-breaker, by demonstrating the will to communicate;
- to inspire an attitude of respect from the indigenous foreign speakers during negotations.

He also views cultural knowledge as vital:
"Some insight into the language builds your confidence and frankly makes it less isolating. Studying the customs of life in Japan is one of the most useful parts of the course. A knowledge of what might happen next, or when to remove your shoes, saves stress and embarrassment and creates a feeling of integrity with the group."

In terms of the **balance of language skills** in demand, most learners want speaking and understanding, particularly in the initial stages. Acquisition of reading skills is also required, though this is realistically attainable only in the longer term at a higher level of proficiency. The ability to write in the foreign language is fourth in importance, though obviously the four skills overlap and are interwoven.

At survival level emphasis is placed on acquiring the ability to cope in hotels, airport lounges (eg the ability to understand flight numbers called out in a foreign language), customs, and railway stations, and in social situations. More advanced learners obviously have a broader spectrum of requirements: Senior Managers and Heads of Departments of some companies travel abroad frequently for conferences and business meetings with foreign companies, or to the HQ of their own company abroad, or to an overseas subsidiary, or they receive overseas businessmen in their company.

Skills required include:

- giving presentations and lectures; holding and attending seminars in the foreign language;

- understanding the informal discussions which take place between formal sessions at a conference;
- starting up a new site abroad, or re-organising a foreign plant or company acquisition;
- communicating with engineers and shop-floor workers on site;
- coping with all these areas on secondment overseas.

Learners also need language skills to face more specific, concrete situations:

- communicating with foreign visitors and HGV drivers from European countries;
- coping with foreign correspondence and telephone calls to and from the foreign country;
- understanding German computer software and speaking to a German computer programmer;
- conducting market research in European countries;
- preparing for an examination to gain an international qualification;
- processing foreign tenders and contracts;
- gist-reading scientific and technical documents in a foreign language;
- acquiring banking and accounting skills in French.

To summarize, the chief objectives of these companies in encouraging their employees to learn foreign languages are: to expand their foreign markets and compete with overseas companies whose employees have more competent language skills; to find new products in other countries and expand their own range; to establish better communication with its subsidiaries overseas or, if it is itself the subsidiary, with the overseas headquarters of its own company. Moreover, the need to learn languages can apply at all levels: from Company Directors, Senior Management and Middle Management to research scientists, engineers, patenting officers, secretaries, telephonists, HGV drivers and security officers on the gate.

Modes Of Tuition

1. Regular Weekly Courses

There are two basic types of regular weekly courses:

- traditional regular weekly on-site courses, generally advertised internally and open to all whose attendance is sanctioned by the company;

- regular weekly language courses designed for a specific group of learners with a specific common objective.

The first type of course is generally on-going and progresses over a number of years from *ab initio* level to highly advanced. The courses are normally one and a half to two hours in duration, and are held in the early morning, over the lunch period or in the late afternoon, so that the minimum amount of company time is taken up. Of great importance is the fact that tuition takes place on site; firstly, because the time factor is costly to the company, and, secondly, because the location is convenient to the learner, who usually has a very tight schedule. One learner, a Development Manager involved in the merchanting part of his company, indicated how the system compared favourably with industrial language training in Germany:

"Tuition on site meant that I could leave the office only a couple of minutes before the class was due to start. When I explain this to my overseas contacts who are learning English, they always state how lucky I am. They tend to have classes at inconvenient times, and may have far to travel."

At the initial stages, where the acquisition of speaking and understanding skills are in the vast majority of cases the main objective, the development of relevant course materials and the use of a communicative teaching methodology are vital. Thus, tuition is in the target language; it is inter-active and practical with much use of pair-work and group-work and situational dialogue, carefully monitored by the tutor. Audio and tapes are always an integral part of every course, and video tapes are used where appropriate.

The drawback is that these courses cannot be designed to meet the specific requirements of each individual member of the group, but it is possible to compensate for this by first analysing individual desires and demands and from time to time using materials and methods based on these for tuition. The specialist skills involved may not be of immediate relevance to every participant, yet all are acquiring the four basic skills of listening, speaking, reading and writing plus some experience of the language of their own field of interest. The success is apparent from the regular take–up by some of the largest companies in the U.K. Courses in German, French, Spanish and Japanese are currently in progress on the site of a major chemical company; courses in Spanish at a large telecommunications company; German, French and Spanish at a major glass manufacturing company, as well as courses in French, German and Spanish at smaller firms.

The second type of regular weekly course is the *closed* course containing a more homogeneous group of learners with a common and specific target. As in every type of course, methodology is communicative and inter–active, and the emphasis is placed upon themes and skills relevant to the business needs of the learners, and progression is cyclical and thematic. Examples of this type of course are:

(i) **German for the Patenting Agents of a large company.** Tuition was for one and a half hours twice weekly over the lunch period. The objective was to obtain an international patenting qualification for which they were required to translate patenting documents from German into English under examination. Although oral skills were not the immediate objective, communicative methodology was used as the most effective means for learning structures and acquiring a lexical base. Materials were specially developed over two years, based on patenting documents, and graded in linguistic complexity. Examination skills were developed by the production of learning materials based on actual examinations, again increasing in structural complexity over the two years.

(ii) **Ab initio Italian for a major chemical concern.** Six groups received 2 hours of tuition a week. Tuition was on site, and the company wanted syllabuses to run parallel at different times with the same tutor, so that participants who occasionally missed classes due to work commitments, could catch up in another group.

The background to the company's request for tuition was a joint venture with an Italian company. This required employees of the British company to attend meetings and conferences with their Italian counterparts in Italy and other countries. Although the official medium of the meetings was English, the company wished to make a friendly gesture to the Italian group. Also, knowledge of Italian would facilitate effective inter-action with Italian colleagues, enable the company's employees to travel independently in Italy and eventually to understand the gist of informal discussions held in Italian at the meetings. In addition, the office workers in the group need to be able to understand telex and telephone messages and queries, ranging from technical data to suitable dates for meetings.

The methods were communicative and inter-active with audio tapes. Tuition was part situational and thematic, based on the exact requirements of the learners, involving simulated social situations which learners would encounter in Italy. Learners were also familiarised gradually with technical terminology in Italian, so they would have the ability to understand at least the gist of the informal discussions held on work topics.

(iii) **Spanish for a small group of senior managers** of a large company with subsidiaries in many overseas countries. The company's strong South American connections involved group travel to Argentina and Mexico. Spanish was required for social and business purposes abroad and receiving business contacts on site. All members of the group had close business contacts at senior management level, and required additional reading skills to cope with correspondence. Here, tuition was geared to the need for communication skills in speaking, understanding and reading, involving the acquisition of relevant technical lexis. Special emphasis was placed on Hispanic customs and on the specialized skills of making formal speeches and discussing production processes in Spanish.

2. Intensive Language Training

Intensive language training, or the 'Crash Course', is found by most language experts to be the least cost-effective and the least efficient mode of language training. Learning a foreign language intensively is stressful, however friendly and relaxed the learning environment, and requires a high level of concentration and commitment. Consequently it is not normally possible to sustain an effective pace and level of input for long periods of time, and this must be taken into account when an intensive package is planned. Design features must be built in to the programme which help counteract the inevitable 'slowing-down' factor evident in intensive learning. These would include:

- variety of teaching materials;
- variety of teaching media (use of audio-tapes, video tapes, language laboratory, film);
- variety of tutor (team teaching);
- combination of native and non-native tutors;
- built-in consolidation sessions;
- friendly and relaxed teaching atmosphere, neither too formal nor too familiar;
- inclusion of a language lunch and language-speaking coffee breaks.

Although every other mode of tuition is more effective in the longer term, in certain circumstances intensive tuition is the only possibility: an unforeseeable need or an emergency might arise at short notice or only a limited block of time is available.

Model Intensive Language Training Package: Case Study

When a request for intensive tuition in German for a male employee of a company was recently received, a language needs analysis was first carried out by Halton College to ascertain the following information:

i) the learner's position within the company;
ii) his experience of the language to date;
iii) his method of acquiring his knowledge;
iv) the language skills already gained (speaking, understanding, reading, writing);
v) what linguistic skills were required;

vi)   for what purposes;

vii) whether a specialised or technical knowledge of the language was needed and for what purpose;

viii) how many hours of tuition were desired and over what period of time;

ix)   whether the client preferred tuition on his own premises or at Halton College.

The information received produced the following profile:

The client was a member of the Senior Management of a local company. He had completed a well-known self-teaching course and had worked through part of a business course.

He had a sound grasp of grammar and was competent in written German. The manager visited Germany regularly on behalf of his company and required proficiency in oral skills and in understanding spoken German. He needed to be able to inter-act socially, to understand proceedings and speak at business meetings, but he did not need "survival" German.

Course Package

The course was to last for 16 hours, from 9 a.m. to 5 p.m. held on two consecutive days at Halton to avoid interruptions.

A co-ordinating meeting was first held with the four tutors, including a native speaker involved in the course. The programme was submitted to them and materials were discussed and selected. The structure of the programme was modified, finalised, and then submitted to the learner.

Materials Selection

Newspaper articles were found with specialized information on his industry. Relevant selections were made from existing business-language learning materials and newspaper articles on current affairs. Audio tapes, video tapes and the language laboratory were used. The syllabus was cyclical and thematic, with emphasis on themes relevant to the learner's conference/business needs, and tuition only in German.

Programme.

Maximum input time was restricted to the morning, which included a small amount of laboratory consolidation time. A carefully constructed language lunch was arranged whose content was based on the morning session, as well as on more informal conversation, and attended by a native speaker and a non-native speaker tutor. The afternoon session consisted of consolidation and use of role-playing and video tape materials. The day was concluded with an evaluation session.

3. Packages With Mixed Modes Of Training

A combination of several modes of tuition is appropriate in complex circumstances. One representative example is a German course prepared for a Services Commissioning Manager who was to be seconded by his company to start up a new complex in Germany. In this case the manager had had the
opportunity to prepare himself for his new role well in advance, and attended first a third-year German course which met once a week. His special need required an additional block of tuition adapted to the future requirements of his job, so Halton prepared a 'Business Appointments' course for him to run concurrently. A block of four hours per week was booked under this flexible system, when tuition took place at varying times, part at Halton and part on site. One tutor and a foreign language assistant were involved. Then, four weeks before his departure for Germany, Halton prepared a semi-intensive training package for him consisting of three hours of tuition each morning for four days a week and at least a similar amount of consolidation work in his own time.

The Value Of Language Training

Measurement in concrete terms of the benefit a company has derived from employees receiving language training is not possible, since the business success of any company in any area can be attributable to a number of different factors. It is, however, possible to evaluate the success achieved by business people with foreign language skills in other ways. For example, our survey clearly shows that the acquisition of "survival" skills helps to prevent mistakes, to correct accidents, to avoid losing the way and to cope better in practical situations. One major advantage of this is to give the businessman greater confidence and a sense of ease at meetings with his foreign counterparts, eliminating a degree of stress. Relations with customers and with business contacts are similarly enhanced if an attempt has been made to communicate in their language and to understand their customs and way of life. As a Marketing Executive expressed it:

"My ability to speak even a limited amount of German has proved useful when discussing business matters, and when my German counterpart realised that I'd taken the trouble to learn how they lived and knew something about their customs, he was amazed. I'm sure this made a positive contribution to our business discussions."

The ability to understand the gist of informal conversations of overseas colleagues at a conference gives insight into proceedings and attitudes as a whole, and gives the reassurance and self-confidence needed for mingling. In a more formal context the possession of language skills at a level which permits a business person to participate in discussions, give an address or presentation or chair a meeting in the foreign language engages the respect of participants and, moreover, facilitates his influence over the meeting's progress, outcome and policy decisions.

Financial advantages are important, too, such as dispensing with the expensive services of translators and interpreters, provided linguistic limitations are known. A member of the Business Group of one company claimed:

"Through knowledge of German I have been able to save my company money by carrying out overseas market research without using expensive agencies, translations or our local company's sales staff. Learning the language is the first stage of understanding foreign cultures, leading to better quality discussions with overseas contacts, good relationships with local company personnel and acceptance as a European – a vital aid to our company's growth."

Several export managers have claimed that their language skills are indispensible if their companies are to compete with overseas companies. As one manager learning Japanese stated:

"Learning Japanese is an important aspect of generating our sales into Japan. Incidentally, our sales are now going well after a very ragged start."

After 8 months of learning German, about 20 employees of one company visited a subsidiary in Germany. "They put us to shame", was the general comment, "their English was perfect. We've a long way to go."

The evidence proves, however, that they were at least moving in the right direction.

Chapter 17

SPECIALIST TRANSLATION IN INDUSTRY AND COMMERCE:
THE PRACTICAL ASPECTS
Dr Noel Anderson

It is clearly important to service both the specialist and non–specialist foreign language requirements of business. While the increase in interest in the needs of industry and commerce may offer some hope that more attention will be paid to solving the non–specialist language problems, the requirements in relation to specialists are likely to prove a tougher nut to crack. It therefore seems appropriate in this chapter to examine one particular problem in this area, i.e. the need for competent specialist translators, the term 'specialist' being understood to cover subjects as varied as science and technology on the one hand, and finance and accounting on the other.

Translation plays a fundamental role in exporting into markets where the local language is not English. The first requirement is for the exporter to have a thorough knowledge of the climate, needs and potential purchasing capacity of the market concerned. This will mean a detailed study not only of the relevant data relating to the market, but also of the competition; both of these activities will normally involve processing a large number of documents, most of them in a foreign language. In the second place, effective advertising material will have to be made available. Finally, for many products it will be necessary to provide operating and servicing instructions in the language of the target country; in the case of plant and machinery, this type of documentation is normally very extensive.

Unless the key personnel in the exporting company have a high degree of competence in the relevant language, all these requirements will engender a considerable amount of translation work, both into and from the foreign language. Normally, the work of translation into the foreign language will be carried out by translators whose mother tongue is the language of the target country. In Britain, for example, it has become fairly standard practice for translators to translate only into their mother tongue or language of habitual use; this practice is not always adhered to in other countries, with results which are often less than satisfactory. Nevertheless, exporting into foreign markets with non–English–speaking populations will also entail translation into English by English native speakers. Much of this work will be highly specialist in nature, e.g. the translation of specifications of plant or equipment, financial documents, or local safety regulations.

The operations of multinationals also give rise to many translation requirements, often across several language interfaces. Thus, for reasons of efficiency, a centre in Germany, for example, may specialise in the manufacture of one type of product and a centre in Britain in another; in each case this will result in a need to translate the advertising material and technical documentation from the local language into other languages. Moreover, there will generally be a need to make technical and company reports available in more than one language.

A point which is often overlooked is that translation can itself become an important export. The reason for this is that a translator based in his own country has certain advantages over his compatriot based in a foreign country, e.g. he is abreast of developments in his own country and with the current usage in his own language, whereas the expatriots' knowledge in both areas is likely to become dated unless he returns home frequently and for longish periods. The home–based translator is also better placed when it comes to sorting out awkward questions of terminology because of easier access to sources of information. His/her language is not prone to become "tainted" with foreign turns of speech as that of ex–patriots frequently does. Translators and translation agencies can turn these circumstances to advantage and export something we have in abundance – our language. In view of the standing of English as an international language, this is a possibility which deserves to be more widely exploited.

The Nature Of Specialist Translation

Specialist translation is an activity which is little understood by those outside the profession. This has unfortunate results in that it is often undervalued and that the criteria used to select translators and translation agencies are often ill–conceived. It also means that specialist translation work is not infrequently attempted by people who do not have the relevant background, which the results are in many cases far from satisfactory, which not only leads to customer dissatisfaction and tends to bring the profession undeservedly into bad repute.

Much of the misunderstanding of the nature of specialist translation stems from the use of translation in schools and on language courses as a method of instruction (a practice which is now fortunately on the wane). The purpose of this type of translation is not to produce translations but to improve language skills, and it is usually quite inadequate for training specialist translators. By contrast, translation in a business context is for real and is not for the improvement of the translator's linguistic skills (which should be in any case high), the purpose being to transmit information from a source language into a target language as part of an information dissemination process. Following a Soviet convention[1], it is useful to describe the first type of translation as 'instructional translation' and the second as 'professional translation'.

It is very important to distinguish between these two types of translation. While instructional translation is concerned **solely** with linguistic knowledge, professional translation, though demanding extensive linguistic skills (e.g. an in–depth knowledge of the source language and an ability to express oneself effectively in the specialist form of the target language*), requires extensive non–linguistic knowledge. Indeed, this non–linguistic knowledge is as crucial a factor in determining the quality of a translation as the translator's linguistic knowledge. To take a very simple example, the German word 'Aufnahme' can have a wide range of meanings depending on context, e.g. 'recording', 'photograph', 'power consumption', 'absorption', 'inclusion', etc. If he encounters this word in a German text, the translator has to have the necessary specialist knowledge to enable him to select the appropriate English equivalent, otherwise his translation will be nonsense. The problems which occur in reality are in fact often very much more complicated and cannot usually be resolved with anything less than a thorough understanding of the subject matter.

The training of a specialist translator must also extend to a variety of other skills, which may include, for example, one or more of the following:

an ability to read drawings and/or electrical circuit diagrams;

---

*An instructive and at the same time entertaining book on the language used by chemists has recently appeared[2].

an ability to understand chemical formulae and equations,
an ability to interpret mathematical equations.

This may seem unnecessary at first sight, but it is important to appreciate that the non–textual material is frequently essential to an understanding of the text itself and that without it, it is sometimes virtually impossible to solve the problem of translation. If this were not so, the non–textual material would not be included. Many ideas cannot in fact be effectively explained without resorting to visual aids. Anyone who doubts this should try to describe a safety pin or 13–amp plug without using diagrams; not only is the task itself difficult, but the reader is likely to have problems in understanding the resulting text.

There are other reasons why the translator has to have specialist knowledge. One is that he may be required to point out errors in the original text, and professional translators will normally do this as a matter of course. The translator is, after all, the only peron who is as intimately concerned with the text as the original author[3].

Another argument for the specialist translator having the appropriate back–ground knowledge is that in some cases he may be required to recast a text to make it more acceptable in a particular country. This is often the case, for example, with user handbooks since account has to be taken of cultural and educational differences between countries. Recasting may also be necessary because linguistic style varies profoundly from one nation to another, and this applies to many kinds of published texts.

Categories Of Specialist Translator

Specialist translators fall into three main categories:

    (a)   company staff translators. i.e. translators working in commercial or industrial companies as permanent members of staff;

    (b)   agency staff translators, i.e. translators employed by agencies on a permanent basis;

    (c)   freelance translators.

These categories are not necessarily strictly defined since staff translators may in some cases also do some freelance work. Indeed, a recent survey indicates that in most countries the majority of translators are freelance. The number employed by agencies seems to be very small.

The company staff translator has, at least in principle, some advantages over his freelance and agency colleagues. Being part of the "client", he has direct access to people with an intimate knowledge of the subject matter of the texts he has to translate. In a manufaturing company he will also have access to the products and to the departments producing them so that he can acquaint himself with them at first hand. In addition, his duties are often wider since he will often be expected to act as an interpreter at meetings and training courses. Experience of this type of work is almost invariably an asset to a translator.

Depending on the quality of the agency, experience as an agency staff translator can also be invaluable. Firstly, the texts will cover a wider range of subjects than in commercial and industrial companies. If the agency employs a number of translators with different specialisms there will be a greater scope for dealing with texts involving more than one field (e.g. electronics and chemistry).

Staff translators of both kinds also have another advantage over their freelance colleagues, viz. provided the agency or company employs more than one translator, they can check each other's work. This is important since checking one's own work is always less efficient. Another approach to this problem is to employ linguist–checkers who, although not technically qualified, are able to check for correspondence between the original and translated texts and, of course, eliminate grammatical and typing errors, thus releasing translators for more specialist work.

Conversely, the freelance translator is at a disadvantage compared with staff translators. Firstly, he usually has less contact with other translators who may be able to offer him advice and guidance. Secondly, if he works through agencies, he is likely to have less opportunity for discussing problems directly with clients and he may receive little or nothing in the way of constructive feedback (this is very important for improving the quality of a translator's work). Thirdly, unless he is prepared to go to considerable expense he is likely to have far fewer facilities than his staff colleagues. Finally, he has to concern himself with important non-linguistic activities such as soliciting work, invoicing, keeping accounts, and a variety of other 'non-productive' activities. He will also have to type his own work or arrange to have it typed.

Training And Selection

It cannot be said that there is at present any established route to specialist translation work. Certainly no one seems to decide to undertake this type of work in childhood, and it is unlikely that a careers adviser could map out a course of training for the profession. Translators seem on the whole to enter their profession more by chance than as part of a well-considered plan. While this may be satisfactory in some cases, it seems desirable, in view of the growing importance of translation, that consideration should be given to the establishment of more formal training courses for specialist translators than the few post-graduate courses that exist at present in Higher Education.

The present unstructured situation makes it difficult to recruit and select translators. Firstly, they usually have to be attracted into translation work from other professions. Secondly, the criteria on which selection can be based are not well established. While there are examinations for translators, success in them is not necessarily a guide to performance; on the one hand, such examinations lay an undue emphasis on linguistic ability, and on the other, the candidate is examined under artificial conditions rather than observed in a working environment. Examinations can give no guide to a candidate's ability to learn from experience, to his conscientiousness and to his ability to perform efficiently in real situations. Examination results cannot therefore form a basis for selection on their own, and test translations are often no more satisfactory. It is therefore necessary to consider not only examination results, but specialist qualifications and experience, as willl as personality and attitude, when selecting translators.

The Future

With the increasing internationalisation of companies, translation is likely to assume a greater role in Britain's business life. It cannot be said that we are at present suitably equipped to meet this challenge . Firstly, there is a lack of competent specialist translators and, secondly, the approach to translation is piecemeal and inconsistent.

There is clearly an urgent need for a better understanding of the nature of technical translation outside the profession. Furthermore, if we are to have sufficient specialist translators with the appropriate skills, there is a need to re-examine the whole issue of formal training courses for translators. There is much to be said for 'apprenticeship' schemes in which those new to the profession can work for a period of time, preferably a year or more, under the guidance of a more experienced translator.

At the same time there is a strong argument for a move away from freelance translation. Many agencies prefer to use freelance translators for economic reasons, viz. staff costs are kept to a minimum and translators can be selected for different jobs on a cost basis (sometimes being played off against each other). However, this system has disadvantages for both the agency and the translator; many freelance translators do not have the facilities to do their job efficiently and the quality of the work is therefore not as high as it should be, which does not reflect well on the agencies themselves. While many clients tend to look primarily at cost when selecting translators and translation agencies, those offering translation services need to place much more emphasis on the quality they can offer. In any case, because of the cost advantages to be gained from the use of shared 'hardware', those agencies which employ staff translators may soon have a distinct advantage over employers of freelance translators in terms of cost, quality and speed of response.

References and Notes

1. Krupnov V.N., *V tvorcheskoi laboratorii perevodchika* (In the creative laboratory of the translator), Moscow, 1976.

2. Schoenfeld R., *The Chemist's English*, VCH Verlagsgesellschaft, Weinheim, 1985.

3. Schmitt P. A., Fachtextübersetzung und "Texttreue": Bemerkungen zur Qualität von Ausgangstexten, *Lebende Sprachen*, (1987), No. 1, pp. 1–7.

4. Smith D.J., The Digital Report on Translation Practice, *Language Monthly*, No. 42 (March, 1987), pp. 11–13.

APPENDIX 1

Survey Of The Use Of Foreign Languages In Northern Industry And Commerce*

Q1 Exports
Approximately what proportion of your goods/services do you sell *directly* to:–

(a) the home market

%

(b) other English–speaking countries (incl. USA and Commonwealth)

%

(c) *Non–English–Speaking–Countries*

%

Q2 Imports
Approximately what proportion of your goods/services do you buy *directly* from:–

(a) the home market

%

(b) other English–speaking countries

%

(c) *Non–English–Speaking Countries*

%

Q3 In the table below please list the *principal Non–English–Speaking Countries, or regions,* you trade with and the *main goods* you buy or sell there. Please use the appropriate industrial Class No. from the list below:

1. agric/forestry
2. mining
3. food/drink/tobacco
4. chemicals/allied

10. instrument/precision eng.
11. electronics
12. textiles/clothing/footwear
13. domestic goods

5. fine chemicals/pharm
    6. ferrous metals
    7. mechanical eng.
    8. electrical eng.
    9. marine/heavy eng.

14. misc. manufacture
15. R & D
16. services
17. other (please specify) . . . . .

. . . .

Trade Table: Exports/Imports

	Countries or Regions	Class No. of goods (see above)	Approx. value of goods (£) in previous year	please tick if you used local agent or interpreter abroad	Language of transaction
Your Exports To:					
Your Imports From:					

Q4 Do you feel there are any countries/regions where you could have significantly improved your trade performance over the last few years with access to foreign language facilities?

Yes [　　] 　　 No [　　]

If so, which languages? | Fr. | | Ger. | | Sp. | |

| Russ. | | It. | | Jap. | | Arab. | |

| Other | | – Please specify ....

Q5 Which *Non–English–Speaking Countries* do you consider potential areas of trade growth for your company over the next few years?
Please specify. ....

Q6 In the boxes below please *tick the principal activities* where your company has used a foreign languages in trade contacts with foreign companies. Please double tick the most important.

1. Wining & dining (social chat) ☐
2. Travelling abroad ☐
3. Using the phone ☐
4. Writing letters/notes ☐
5. Writing trade documents ☐
6. Reading letters/telex ☐
7. Listening to talks ☐
8. Reading tech./sales lit. ☐
9. Giving talks/speeches ☐
10. Other (please specify) ....
    ....

Q7 Have you bought in the services of an outside translation/interpreting bureau here or abroad during the past 3 or so years?

| Yes, here | | No | |

If 'yes', for which languages?

| Fr. | | Ger. | | Sp. | | Russ. | |

| It. | | Arab. | | Jap. | |

| Other | | – Please specify ....

Q8 For which languages have you used your own staff (or Head Office) for foreign contacts over the past 3 or so years?

Fr.		Ger.		Sp.		Russ.	

It.		Arab.		Jap.	

Other | | – Please specify . . . .

Q9 Please give: Your name/position company address

County | | Post Code

Q10 What was your approximate turnover last year? £ | |

Q11 Address of Head Office (if different)

Name & Address of Controlling Co. (if subsidiary)

Thank you for your cooperation. For any queries contact –
Mr Stephen Hagen, Project Director, Newcastle Polytechnic.

APPENDIX 2

Questionnaire On Industrial/Commercial Use Of Oriental & African Languages*

1. Have you used any of the following languages in the last few years? (Please rank in order of importance)

    Arabic ☐   Japanese ☐   Chinese ☐   Korean ☐

    – Any other Oriental or African?
    Please list ....
    ....

2. (i)   Please list those of the above languages for which you used your own staff: ....
    ....
    (ii) Please list those of the above languages for which you used a translation bureau: ....
    ....
    (iii) Please list those of the above languages for which you used a local agent: ....
    ....

3. Could you increase, or could you have increased, your trade performance with access to expertise in the following languages (please prioritise):

    Arabic ☐   Japanese ☐   Chinese ☐   Korean ☐

    Other Oriental/African languages? ....
    ....

*This is an abridged version of the original questionnaire, it is copyright and permission to use any part of it should be addressed to the author, Stephen Hagen.

4. Please complete the table with those Oriental/African languages which your company may use for these business activities:

Languages

reading telex/letters	
negotiation	
travel	
trade fair	
social chat	
translation (written)	
translation (oral)	
Please list others ...	

5. Where would you go for services in Oriental/African Languages (please prioritise): local University of Poly/private language school/business school/ business club/Chamber of Commerce/ BOTB/Other   (Please delete)

6. Name of company ....

   Approximate Annual Turnover

   Any comments (Continue overleaf if necessary) ....

APPENDIX 3

Regional GDP per head as a percentage of the UK(1) average

	1985	Rank Position 1975	Rank Position 1984	Rank Position 1985
North of England	92.9	7	8	7
Yorkshire & Humberside	91.8	6	9	9
East Midlands	95.7	5	3	5
East Anglia	100.7	8	2	2
South East	114.7	1	1	1
South West	93.9	9	5	6
West Midlands	92.3	2	7	8
North West	96.0	4	6	4
Wales	88.9	10	10	10
Scotland	97.4	3	4	3
Northern Ireland	74.8	11	11	11

(1) UK excludes profits attributable to the Continental Shelf.

Source: *Northern Economic Review,* Winter 1986/7, No 14, p.54.

Notes

The relative prosperity of a region can be measured by a comparison of its GDP per head with the UK average. In 1985 the South East was the only region significantly above the UK average, though East Anglia is now slightly over the 100 mark which it first achieved on revised figures for 1984. It is still the case, however, that in terms of GDP per head the South East is well ahead of other regions in Great Britain.

BIBLIOGRAPHY

Ager, D.E. (1985) Languages in your future. *Modern Languages,* Sept No.3, pp161–165.

Bungay, S. (1986) Horse–dealing in Europe in: *German in the United Kingdom,* pp16–20

'CBI calls for more European Languages', *Education,* 3/7/87.

Collinson, M., Hanage, P., Readman, P.W., and Wilkinson, J. (1982) Foreign Languages in Business in Cleveland 1981. Supply, Demand and Application. Unpublished DMS dissertation, Teeside Polytechnic.

Coutts, J.W. (1981) A Pilot Investigation into the Foreign Language Needs of International Trade. Unpublished MA dissertation, London University.

Dixon, M. (1987) Language Courses, *Financial Times,* 21 February 1987, p.XV

Dixon, M. (1987) Why English is good, but not good enough. *Financial Times,* 21 February 1987, p.XVI

Emmans, K., Hawkins, E. and Westoby, A. (1974) Foreign Languages in Industry/Commerce, Language Teaching Centre, University of York.

"Even the British find it pays to learn languages", *The Economist,* 16–22 May, 1987, pp71–72.

Finlay, I.F. (1981) Working with Languages. The Institute of Linguists Educational Trust, London.

Firth, R.A., Carney, B. and Dane, M. (1984) Using Languages, AGCAS Careers Information Booklet, CSU, Manchester.

Gold, K. (1985) Few takers for a rich menu, *Times Higher Educational Supplement,* 26 June 1987, p.11

Graham, C. (1987) Industry and Foreign Languages. DES–PICKUP

Report, June 1987.

Hagen, S. (1985) Trading in other tongues, *Times Higher Education Supplement*, 10 May, p.16.

Hagen, S. (1986) German – the first foreign language of Northern English Industry, in: *German in the United Kingdom – Issues and Opportunities*, CILT Reports and Papers 24, London.

Hagen, S. (1986) North Loses Trade for lack of Foreign Languages *Target*, Tyne and Wear Chamber of Commerce, 5, Jan, p2.

Hagen, S. (1987) The Changing World of Languages in Industry and Commerce in: Kingston, P.J. (ed) pp79–81.

Hantrais, L. (1985) Using Languages in a Career, Aston University Modern Languages Club.

Hoffman, R.J.S. (1983) *Great Britain and the German Trade Rivalry 1875–1914*, New York: Garland.

Holden, N. (1983) The Japanese Language: A partial view from the inside *Multilingua* 2–3, pp157–166.

Hurman, J. (1982) Modern linguists: industrial demand and school supply – a survey and a proposal, *Modern Languages*, LXIII (1), pp.44–8.

Jones, F. (1986) Industry held back by lack of languages, *T.E.S*, 23 May, p6.

Kingston, P.J. (ed) (1987) Languages – The Challenge of Change. Selected Proceedings of JCLA Conference, University of Hull.

Knowles, F. (1982) Foreign languages – what do we expect? *Modern Languages*, LXIII (2), pp.97–103

Lee, E.V. (1977/8) Non–specialist use of foreign languages in industry and commerce, *Audio–Visual Language Journal*, XV (3), pp.223–31

Liston, D. and Reeves, N. (1985) *Business Studies, Languages and*

Overseas Trade: A Study of Education and Training, Plymouth and London: Macdonald and Evans and the Institute of Export.

Mellors, C., Copperthwaite, N. (1985) Using a European studies degree. *Modern Languages,* September, (3), pp166–174.

Morris, C. (1980) Are modern languages of any use? A limited survey of job opportunities for modern linguists, *Modern Languages,* LXI (3), pp.109–12

Newcastle Polytechnic (1977,1984) *Directory of Employers in the Northern Region,* Appointments and Careers Advisory Service, 1977, 1983 (Revised 1984)

North of England Development Council (1986) *North of England Focus on Investment,* Newcastle upon Tyne.

Quirk, R. (1987) English is not enough. *T.H.E.S,* 11/12/87, p13.

Research and Intelligence Unit, Cleveland County Council (1986/7) Statistical Review, *Northern Economic Review,* No.14 pp54–64

Reeves, N. (1986) Why German? in: *German in the United Kingdom,* pp 1–12.

Reeves, N. (1985) Educating for Exporting Capability – Languages and Market Penetration, *The Incorporated Linguist,* 24, No.3/4 pp147–153.

Savage, R.F. (1980) Modern Languages in Education and Industry in Staffordshire. Unpublished Report, Staffordshire County Council.

'S'il vous pay', *The Economist,* 21 June, 1986, p30–31.

Skapinker, M. (1986) Why speaking English is no longer enough, *International Management,* Nov, pp.39–42

Statham, N. (1981) Review of the Problem, in: *The Language Key in Export Strategy* pp7–14.

Steadman, H. (1984) A String to your Bow, *Graduate Post* (26), 9 March 1987, pp.13–14.

Steadman, H. (1985) Language – the key to export marketing, *Executive Post*, 4 Oct. p1.

Stewart, W. (1986) Dumb Stupidity, *Today*, 16 June, p10.

'Trade Chiefs in crisis talks on Russian shortage', *T.H.E.S*, Headline, 4/12/87 p1.

Wilding, C. (1980) Languages and Education and Industry: A Summary of Reports and Conferences, Birmingham: Aston University

Wilding, C. (1979/80) Unpublished Survey through the Careers Office of the University of Aston, Birmingham: University of Aston.

'Yes, but which language?' *Overseas Trade,* (Letters), Sept 1986.

REPORTS

"Foreign Languages for Overseas Trade: a Report by the BOTB Study Group on Foreign Languages", BOTB, 1979.

"Language for All", Further Education Unit, London, July 1986.

"Europe, Our Future. 1992: A European Area without Frontiers", Commission of the European Communities, June 1987.

"Communication in the International Business World. An Exchange of Experience", Aston University: AMLC, 1985.

"Foreign Languages in the School Curriculum. A draft Statement of Policy", DES, Welsh Office, June 1986.

"Language and Languages 16–19", National Congress on Languages in Education, Papers and Reports 7, 1986.

"German in the United Kingdom. Issues and Opportunities", CILT Reports and Papers 24, London, 1986.

"The Language Key in Export Strategy", University of Aston and BOTB, October 1981.

"European Survey 1979", The Council of British Chambers of Commerce in Europe. June, 1979.

"The Non-Specialist Use of Foreign Languages in Industry and Commerce," LCCI Examinations Board. Revised Edition 1985.

"York Report", See Emmans *et al* (1974).

"A Policy Statement", The British Chamber of Commerce France, Autumn 1979.

"Export Attitudes in the United Kingdom", The British Chamber of Commerce France, June 1979.